THE INVISIBLE ORGANIZATION

How Ingenious CEOs Are Creating Thriving, Virtual Companies

By Mitch Russo

Dedication

This book is dedicated to my dear departed friend Chet Holmes, who has been on this life journey with me since we first met in 1988. Chet died of leukemia complications in August of 2012. In the months following his passing, I decided to write this book.

Table of Contents

Foreword by Jay Abraham

What a wonderful environment to be starting or growing a business. When I started, computers were tens of thousands, reaching people was costly, building formidable organizations took years, costing millions, requiring huge management teams and facilities coast-to-coast. Not anymore. Mitch Russo provides a rather refreshing new slant on growing a business to double, redouble, maybe even double again and again – without heavy fixed investment in people, equipment and costs. He has blueprinted an exceptionally impressive process many people can use to propel rapid growth. Not right for everyone, Mitch's strategy delivers a serious read and even more serious reflection by any CEO who is stuck in a no-growth mode or dealing with limited resources.

Endorsements for
The Invisible Organization

"Mitch Russo busts the biggest myths about jumpstarting your business and reveals what some of the savviest CEOs have been doing behind the scenes that you may have never imagined was possible! *The Invisible Organization* is a must-read only when you're ready to make the commitment to create your overhead-free selling machine."

Mark Thompson, N.Y. Times Bestselling Author, Charles Schwab's former CEO & Cofounder, Virgin Entrepreneurship Centers

Mitch Russo offers an insightful and pragmatic review of what it takes to create an Invisible Organization. Based on his first-hand experience building successful companies with minimal infrastructure, Mitch shares a powerful formula for rapid growth and amazing speed. His simple strategy is equal parts personal leadership, enabling technology, and human capital. People say Wayne Gretzky was great because he could "skate to where the puck is going to be." If you want to run a great organization, Mitch is offering you a clear view of where you'll need to be.

Rick Miller, former President AT&T Global Services and current CEO BeingChief.com

"Turning your company or parts of it into a virtual operation will save you money and increase your profits. Mitch Russo "Nails It" in his book "The Invisible Organization," by telling you step by step how to do it!"

Kevin Harrington, Founder of "As Seen on TV" Inc and "Shark" on the ABC television series Shark Tank.

Acknowledgements

This book was inspired by Jay Abraham. Jay was my mentor for twenty years as I attended his conferences and purchased his incredible courses. No one thinks like Jay, and I immediately felt I found someone who communicated what I needed to hear. I used his ideas to create and sharpen my own ideas. In 2001 our paths crossed in a different way when I hired him and Chet Holmes to help me market a new venture-backed furniture web site.

I had the privilege of working with Jay over the course of several weeks to create a plan and implement it. Years later in 2009 we met face-to-face in the "green room" before Jay spoke at our Ultimate Business Mastery Summit with Tony Robbins. Our friendship was reinforced when Jay and I worked together to solve a problem between him and Chet, which ended in a very positive outcome for both parties.

Jay's way of thinking and the countless examples of business models he provided me to study, contributed greatly to the success of my software company.

When Chet Holmes passed away and I left his company, Jay told me, "It would be a waste if all your knowledge and experience were lost," and he was right.

Like many projects, *The Invisible Organization* started as an idea and later morphed into a book. It's been through several major revisions and enhancements. I would like to thank the following people for helping me perfect my message:

- Shamayah Sarrucco, who is my writing collaborator. She helped me focus my thoughts and turn them into a book I am proud of.

- Robert Michon, who helped me clarify my message and offered much insight into areas that needed more work.

- Rosina Fischer, who helped me update some of the concepts and reminded me where some of my great ideas came from.

- David Kasabian, my longtime friend and editor who has been helping me write more powerful, grammatically correct prose.

- Lonny Hallsted, who inspired me to push this manuscript to the next level.

- Dov Gordon, for his cutting insight into clarity and purpose.

To my darling Carol, who has been the light of my life. Thank you, my love, for all your support while I snuck off to my office to write.

Finally, to my daughter Alessandra, who has been my most powerful inspiration in everything I've done, and who is now working on her own third novel. Thank you, Alessandra. I'm proud of you.

Introduction

You've built a business, and you have done well.

You were leading the pack. Maybe you still are.

But others are catching up. Your customers now have more options. Your products were once considered fantastic and innovative, but it's become harder and harder to come up with new breakthroughs.

If you are like most CEOs, your success and growth brought you new problems. You may have solved them by adding support people and infrastructure.

For a while, things got back on track.

But it wasn't long before profits declined, and your management headache increased. You've come a long way, your organization is bigger, but now there's more friction in a previously simple business.

Which leaves you asking, "How do I restore the vibrancy, excitement and profitability we used to enjoy?"

Or maybe you have enjoyed successful growth but have now reached a plateau, and somehow you seem to be stuck. You wonder, "What can I do to take my company to the next level?"

The answer, my friend, is simple: make your organization *Invisible*!

Are you interested in finding out what you can do to achieve a 500% increase in profits and consistent double-digit growth, all without adding expensive overhead to your existing operations?

What if, over the course of the next several months, you could create and implement a plan that would reduce the friction between you and your clients, your staff and even your vendors while at the same time creating higher profits, more time and exponential growth?

It may sound too good to be true. Yet the reality is that such changes are already happening all over the world in companies large and small. Savvy CEOs are creating and managing frictionless organizations with happier staff, a growing client base, and a low-cost work environment. Wouldn't it be great if your company could be like that, too? It's completely possible.

I personally built one of the world's largest business coaching and training companies, with over 300 people at its peak and generating over $25M per year in revenue, all from a spare bedroom.

Nobody likes friction at the workplace. Unfortunately, it's part of life in most companies. Friction is needless work that occupies time, sucks the productivity out of your staff, and makes everyone take multiple steps to accomplish easy tasks that should have been automated long ago.

In an Invisible Organization, friction can be practically eliminated because each staff member is independent and working from home.

With integrated, consistent and powerful systems, information is instantly available, making work processes effortless, simple and quick.

Your clients will have a delightful and satisfying experience with your company. They will enjoy the ease and joy of your staff's service, and they will value that your company delivers what it promises. Clients will stay clients for many years and will happily refer their friends and family.

If you are committed to excellence, growth, and profits, let's change the world—your world in particular, with this book as your road map. The time is now!

The Invisible Organization is the new business paradigm that defines how frictionless, virtual, overhead-free organizations can be set up, managed and grown to better serve your clients, staff and shareholders.

The Invisible Organization is a philosophical and practical means of optimizing both the work experience and the customer experience by eliminating the friction of the physical world in terms of commuting, time clocks, and expenses/maintenance of in-house equipment.

The Invisible Organization is not a casual "spend one day a week working from home" program. *The Invisible Organization* is designed to transition a company, large or small, to a completely virtual operation with no buildings, coffee machines, desks or parking spaces. Instead of gathering in meeting rooms, teams connect on webinars, Skype, Google Hangouts and other virtual platforms designed to enhance the team-communication experience. All your staff will be working from home, and that will make them happier and more productive than ever before.

The Invisible Organization has fully integrated, highly efficient systems, standardized training, reduction or elimination of physical infrastructure, and very happy staff members who love their company and enjoy their jobs.

Who is this book for?

Whether you are the business owner, the CEO, one of the executives or a visionary employee, keep reading. If you have been searching for a solution to expand without overhead and employ new strategies to increase profits and productivity, you will find this book very useful.

You'll soon discover what is possible and how easy it is to become *invisible*. With the information in this book and some good preparation, expenses can be reduced significantly, sales can be expanded, and profits can explode by setting up home-based staff one division at a time and implementing these powerful new strategies.

If your company needs a facility to meet clients face-to-face or can't be 100% virtual for another reason, the following pages will show you how to become as productive as possible in your circumstances.

Even if, right now, you never plan on sending a single employee home to work, the strategies, tools and processes explained in this book will increase efficiency in any division or department.

Now is the time to make changes so that long-term results can be realized.

Because managing an Invisible Organization is different than a traditional one, I will show you what to measure, how to deal with staff who are not a good fit and, most importantly, how to attract the best people in the world who will appreciate the chance to work with your company.

This book is based on my thirty-five years of experience building, growing, and running multi-million dollar companies. The methods, technology, and philosophy contained within this book have been proven to get results time and time again. And these strategies can be applied to any business, regardless of whether you've just started or have been in business for many years.

Why am I qualified to write about this?

I have been a CEO using these exact concepts on a daily basis to implement every strategy in this book and more.

Before my current company, I ran one of the most successful training and business coaching/consulting organizations in the world from my spare bedroom.

Please know that the values and processes in this book are for any company, as they will improve the efficiency and assist the CEO in increasing profitability.

What will this book do for you?

- Strong, visionary leadership is required to transition a traditional organization into an invisible one. You'll want your staff's buy-in to the process, and you'll have to deal with the inevitable challenges you will encounter.

- You will understand how your mindset as a leader greatly affects the success of going invisible.

- Carefully selected, well-trained, confident staff makes building your company much easier. When your staff members are happy with their jobs, your clients will benefit and so will you.

- You will discover how to hire the most qualified and happiest people in the world to work for you and how to use automated learning environments to train your staff properly.

- Your decision-making will improve, because you will see everything that is going on more clearly than ever before. You will have real-time data on every aspect of your company operations—sales, marketing, traffic, and training stats—as well as access to very granular information on productivity throughout your whole organization.

You will learn what systems you need and how to put them in place. Nothing will be extremely hard to implement, and technology costs will require minimal investment.

- Your profits will rise because you'll stop wasting money on infrastructure that is simply not required.

This book will change how you think about your company and provide you with the model to work from, along with the best ideas and tools I know. You can take advantage of what I present and make your business thrive, or you can keep doing what you are doing now. It's your choice.

Very soon you could be running *your* own Invisible Organization from the comfort of your home or any beach in the world. Be bold and start to take the necessary steps to get your business on the road to phenomenal success today. You will not only feel a sense of personal satisfaction and reward, but your family and your staff members will thank you!

Dig in! I have a lot to share with you.

Mitch Russo

SECTION ONE:

What Some of the Most Ingenious CEOs Have Been Doing Behind the Scenes

Revive Your Business

Shed Overhead, Thrill Your Clients and Boost Productivity

The whole world is moving in this direction. Your competitors may already be working virtually at some level. Some companies have tried and failed, others are succeeding and winning. You may already have a few people who work from home. That's great, but it's just a start. Transitioning to an Invisible Organization requires much more, and the rewards are much greater than you are aware of.

Why is it worth the effort to build an Invisible Organization? You can create more free time, higher profits, greater business success, and probably best of all, *greater fulfillment* for you and your staff. You might not realize it, yet the future of your very business may depend on it.

It's not hard, but it does take determination and the willingness to rethink the way your company operates. The steps I provide are simple and direct regardless of what type of company you have or what industry you are in. I've done it myself, and I've helped others do it—with tremendous results. Now it's your turn.

The goal of this book:

To get you into action quickly so that you can begin the process and enjoy the benefits of a successful Invisible Organization sooner rather than later.

The process will require you to master several new skills and strategies which will be the keys to unlimited business success. You'll be challenged to find ways to become "invisible" in all areas of your company.

You're going to evaluate every department, each staff member and every system you're using now from a different perspective. You'll discover ways to work more efficiently, and as a direct result, *expand your business*. This process will take some time, but the cumulative results will be undeniable. *You will create maximum results with minimum effort and cost.*

Inevitably, this will enable you to *increase* your income.

When asked how they run their sales organization, some business owners might say, "We just pick up the phone, call a prospect and ask for the order." That answer is no longer good enough. You need to break down *exactly* what it is you do into a series of steps that you follow with every single client or customer.

When you know exactly what it is your company is doing, you can *tell* a person exactly what it is you do with *confidence*. This leads to more business because people *like* systems. If they're looking for someone to help them with a specific problem or service, they feel comfortable knowing that there's a tried-and-tested series of techniques in place to get that job done.

Besides selling with confidence, good systems will make expansion easier and training more precise. They will let you build in and repeat successful processes. You can set up the training for your staff and track their results and improve them. You'll know how long it takes to accomplish each action.

Once clearly defined systems are in place, you'll then be able to easily discover ways to maximize your exposure with more effective marketing.

Your marketing system is a *crucial* piece of your business that will ultimately be generating income for you on its own. It will become a major component of your Invisible Organization.

The following chapters will share marketing techniques that go beyond the now-common Facebook and Google ads. These techniques will become huge profit generation systems when used in an Invisible Organization. If you already have great marketing systems in place and want to expand sales while cutting expenses, you are in the right place, too. I'll show you how you can increase productivity and profits while improving the lifestyle of the CEO, the management team, and your staff.

How do I know this for sure? I did it myself. Now I want to help you do it as well.

As the CEO of Business Breakthroughs International, I built a multi-hundred-person organization spanning seven countries and with over 10,000 clients. We doubled our business three years in a row and managed twelve divisions, seven of which had their own Profit and Loss Statement and were profitable. At its peak we generated over $25 million in revenue per year with over five hundred clients every month. On average we had more than fifty working coaches and nearly 100 salespeople, all of them working from the comfort of their own homes. We didn't own a single copy machine, and yet anyone who dealt with us thought we occupied a huge facility with a lot of parking spaces.

The company started as Chet Holmes International and evolved into Business Breakthroughs when Tony Robbins became our joint venture partner.

We collectively assisted thousands of companies with high-level consulting services, coaching and education. I created several new divisions, all profitable almost from day one.

I ran the entire organization as President and CEO from a home office, my spare bedroom converted to a workspace. It was comfortable, easy to work from, and it saved me countless hours and dollars I would have spent maintaining a professional, outside facility. Even though my personal assistant was 2,000 miles away, we functioned as a great team.

Before that, I was a CEO consultant and a venture investor. In that role, I saw hundreds of business models and directly participated in several as an operating executive.

Back in 1985, I built, ran, and sold the most popular time accounting software company ever built called Timeslips Corporation. At one point, Timeslips Corp had over 250,000 clients. We sold that business for over $10M.

With an Invisible Organization you won't need the physical infrastructure you are currently using. Just imagine how much money you could save if you no longer had to pay for rent and utilities. Your first response may be, "That won't work for our company." But think about it. Wouldn't it be a great way to boost profits and create leverage for your business if it *were* possible?

How much money could you really save? Let's take a look.

A small architect's office in Ashland Massachusetts has 12 employees. One is the CEO, another the bookkeeper, another is receptionist, and there is one tech to support the infrastructure. The remaining eight are engineers and draftsman. They have a 4,000-square-foot office space with a conference room, a reception area, and ten individual offices. After understanding their concerns about maintaining their "presence" in the area, I recommended the following, as their lease was up for renewal:

Current Monthly Costs:

Rent at $32/SqFt:	$10,666
Electricity	$816
Gas for Heat	$437
Leased Servers Onsite	$2,850
Custodial	$300
Coffee Service	$195
Snacks	$150
Phone System Lease	$532
Internet	$450
Phone Service	$295
Property and Facilities Insurance	$310
Total:	$17,001 per month

After the CEO decided it was time to become "invisible," most of these costs were eliminated. The company down-sized to an 850-sqare-foot office, which allowed the CEO to maintain his presence with the receptionist. This included a full conference room and two guest workstations with the equipment the company already owned.

The CEO returned his leased server to the leasing company and signed a contract for a cloud-based server, eliminating 3/4 of the company's monthly expenses (and that included new equipment at his hosting company every two years with 24/7 tech support and backup). He sent his entire engineering staff home and gave them each $75 a month to pay for their Internet fees. They were delighted to save money on fuel and lunches, plus they were happy that they didn't have to commute an average of 80 minutes anymore.

After going invisible, the company's monthly costs were:

Rent at $36/SqFt	$2,550
Electricity	$327
Gas for Heat	$196
Coffee Service	$48
Snacks	$54
Internet	$250
Phone Service	$96
Property Insurance	$144
Remote Server Lease	$650
Added Internet for Staff	$750
Total:	$5,065 per month

That's an $11,936-per-month savings—about $143,232 per year—because they converted from a physical location to a virtual organization. Besides the savings, everyone loved working from home, except one engineer who didn't have the self-discipline and had to be let go. As a result productivity soared, the quality of work increased dramatically, and people were logged into their servers from home at all hours of the day and night, willing to work extra if needed without complaint.

Just imagine how much you would save on office furniture, partitions, phone sets, phone systems, and in most cases, even the cost of computers. Since you won't maintain any of your own hardware anymore, you will no longer need a tech support person. Instead you'll rely on your cloud system's provider for help.

In the above example, profits soared and staff became more productive even before we started implementing the really cool stuff: interconnecting all their systems, building their document vault, and creating their automated training environment. That's the next step, and that's where your world will change when it comes to scalability.

Today's cutting-edge systems will open doors you didn't even know existed. Even if you own a manufacturing plant, or operate a medical center, or need manual labor, there are still certain departments that could operate virtually. When you have the proper training systems in place with clear policies and procedures, you can send your sales and administrative team home while watching their productivity increase. They will be happier and will keep more of their net pay.

It's best to transition gradually. Start with just a few people to get used to how it works. Then begin to migrate, and watch the magic happen. Everything I've discussed in this book can be done without physical infrastructure.

Why Stanford says you should send your people home

Increased productivity is a major benefit of an Invisible Organization. Even though some people enjoy the social interaction at the water cooler and the hour lunch break, many prefer to be home so they can make their own food, save money and time, and take care of personal matters instead of chatting with their coworkers during their break.

Stanford University's Landmark Study, "Does Working from Home Work?" published on August 18, 2014, states on page three:

"First, the performance of the home workers went up dramatically, increasing by 13% over the nine months of the experiment. This improvement came mainly from a 9% increase in the number of minutes they worked during their shifts (i.e., the time they were logged in to take calls). This was due to reductions in breaks, time off and sick-days taken by the home workers. The remaining 4% improvement came from home workers increasing the number of calls per minute worked. In interviews, the workers attributed this gain to the greater convenience (the ease of getting tea, coffee, lunch or using the toilet) and quiet of working from home. Second, there appear to be no spillovers to the rest of the group. Comparing the control group to similar workers … we see no performance drop despite the control group's having lost the treatment lottery. (note: The "control group" is the group which was not sent home and used as the comparison to the those sent home to work.) Third, attrition fell sharply among the home workers, dropping by 50% versus the control group. Home workers also reported substantially higher work satisfaction and had more positive attitudinal survey outcomes. Fourth, one downside of WFH appears to be that, conditional on performance, it reduced rates of promotion by about 50%."

Important Point to Remember:

When employing staff members working from home, there is no personality involved when it comes to judging their suitability for continued employment. Only performance counts. Nothing but results determines status, pay, promotion, or bonus. This is quite different than most existing organizations since getting to know your staff members undoubtedly influences all aspects of the choices made for promotion or advancement. As I am sure you are aware, some staff members seem to be busy all the time but are light on results. When only performance and results matter, only your best will be rewarded, your best people now become your core team.

Forget the work day, it's the work experience!

In all the years I've hired staff to work from home, very few wish they could commute to an office. Just look at their savings: there is no cost for fuel, no time spent in the car, no risk of accidental damage or injury while commuting, less trash from fast food, and there's no expensive restaurants for lunch. There's no dry cleaning, no wardrobe costs, and even the threat of catching a cold is reduced! And what about that soul sucking commute on public transportation or spewing thousands of pounds of filth into the atmosphere as traffic jams now move further and further out into the suburbs.

Your home-based staff is focused on their most valuable final product, whatever that is for them, and your new virtual systems track their time and productivity. As long as they meet their quota or staff the phones as required and do so with a great attitude, you are more than satisfied, right? Besides, your staff will feel you trust them by "allowing" them to work from home. No matter how much money you save, they save, too, and that's after-tax money they get to keep. You'll be rewarded with a more conscientious staff, a better work product, and a lower stress, happier person working for you.

For example, with shift-based telephone call centers, home-based workers can take short breaks and walk the dog or run an errand, then log back on when they return. They will love their jobs and the privileges that come with them. If your staff is happier and more productive, your clients will be happier, too. Studies show that most people who work from home will work more hours, be more focused on their tasks, and perform at a higher level than before.

It's as if you gave everyone on staff a big fat raise, yet all the while you've shifted many of your company expenses to your staff individually, as the cost comparison above shows.

Look at it this way: if JetBlue and Southwest Airlines can send their entire call center staff home, it might be worth taking a hard look at your own situation, as long as you have a clear plan and the vision to see your conversion through to the end result.

Companies like JetBlue and Southwest Airlines have embraced the concept of the Invisible Organization and have thousands of reps working from home, monitored by sophisticated systems and attentive managers, all with one goal: to handle more clients more quickly than last month while maintaining a high level of customer service and delivering what's promised every day.

Last month, I booked a flight with JetBlue. After a quick and easy transaction, I asked the pleasant woman on the other end of the phone a simple question.

I asked, "What's it like working from home?"

She paused, not wanting to reveal that she actually did. I added, "I work from home, too."

She immediately loosened up and started to talk. She told me how it's been a blessing in her life, how it saves her money on gas, clothes, eating out, dry cleaning and coffee. She said, "I get to eat my own food, and I can walk my dog when I need to!"

We talked a bit more about how productive she has become. She explained, "I actually take more calls and work more hours but it feels like I am working less because I don't have to commute, and I know I am not contributing as much to global warming."

She seemed genuinely excited to be telling me this. As you will see, as much as this young lady loves to work from home, her employer loves it even more. The money they save on running a multi-hundred-person call center (several of them, actually) around the country is astronomical—no building, no electricity, no equipment, lower insurance, and think about all those cars *not* polluting the environment!

Our conversation lasted about five more minutes, during which time she let me know just how much she loved her company and her job.

Behind the Scenes of an Invisible Organization

Visualize a central hub with hundreds of lines extending to homes all over America. At the top of that hub are your incoming phone lines. Those phone lines come from your 800-number provider and in some cases can be the same company as your virtual call center company. (This is explained in detail in chapter 5.)

As all those lines flow into the hub, the calls are sent to reps at home that are logged into the system waiting for the next call. When they receive a call, a (software) screen pop-up displays the caller's information. That same information automatically populates your CRM database and a new prospect record is created. As the sales rep takes the caller through the sales script that's running onscreen, notes are made and entered into the CRM system.

Your system also automatically receives the caller's telephone number, which is correlated to the radio spot (or any other promotional activity) that ran on a particular station at a particular time. This allows you to measure very effectively how well each marketing initiative is working. Later you can use this information to better select spots, stations, times and geographic areas of the country to improve your results.

The only "administration" work your rep actually does is to ask a few questions and engage the prospect in an inspiring conversation leading to a sale. Even the script can be set up on-screen so that your sales rep is just asking questions and responding based on the caller's answers. This is how an Invisible Organization operates behind the scenes.

The possibilities of how to build an Invisible Organization are wide open, based on the type of business you have. Obviously, if you are a manufacturing organization, it might not be possible to have your entire company go invisible. But your sales and marketing can most certainly "go invisible." There are a few specific types of businesses where not all staff can be virtual, but even that might soon change. Airline pilots may one day be flying planes virtually. Soon most public transportation may be operated virtually.

If you are a dentist or a lawyer, you may think that you can't change how you operate. Yet if you run multiple locations or would like to expand your practice, keep reading. Most of the management techniques and interconnected systems described in this book are very important for your future success.

While restaurants can't transition to operating virtually, learning the concepts of the Invisible Organization is still valuable for restaurant owners. For example, staff could be partially trained in automated training environments long before they step foot in the restaurant. Additionally, all contracts and schedules can be managed, including shift management and reservation tracking.

So even though there are a several types of companies that must stay in the physical workspace, many principles in this book can still be applied to a certain extent.

By now, you probably see how your whole business life can change by restructuring your organization slowly, with little risk and the potential for great rewards. Let's go further and remove any roadblocks to getting it done.

SECTION TWO

Myths, Realities and Outcomes

2

Busting the Myths that Hold you Back

The idea of working remotely isn't new—people have been working from home for decades. But until recently there was no such thing as an *Invisible Company*. When a company is invisible it has no corporate office, no fixed assets like desks, chairs, partitions, etc., and no overhead. Instead there is a well-trained staff in place with proven systems and procedures that make the work flow effortlessly in order to serve the clients best.

When new paradigms are first introduced, the general population has a tendency to resist change. They want to keep things the way they've always been. Yet the early adopters are the ones who ride the front of the wave and reap the greatest rewards. Something new and unknown often causes myths and misconceptions to take root. In this section I'll shine light on them, so you'll have a better vision of what is truly possible.

This isn't a technology book. It's a mind-shift jolt designed to transform *you* first and then your *company*. From my own experience I can tell you that success is rarely about the tech you have. The core of your company's success lies in the people involved: you, your staff, and your clients. This book will cover technology requirements, yes, but it will do so from the CEO's perspective without drilling down to the ones and zeros of it all.

Myth #1: It won't work for my company.

Initially the thought of having all your staff work from home might be considered a management nightmare, but as you will see, the path has already been blazed. Many companies have moved some, if not all, of their staff out of their corporate headquarters.

If you don't see how this could work for you, remember that it's not an all-or-nothing game. This is about seeking best practices and moving forward with them at the pace and to the extent that works for your particular company.

Even if you've tried to do this before and failed, don't think it can't be done successfully. Things are different now. The road has been paved, and the signposts are brightly lit to show you the way. If you've failed before, you probably didn't have all the knowledge required to succeed. Now with this book, you will see exactly how to become invisible efficiently and quickly without making the traditional mistakes that might have contributed to your failure in the past.

Everyone who is successful has failed, probably several times. Most of us still have those "scars," and they might make us reluctant to try something new again. Negative feelings may come up when big transitions are about to be made. When you can spot them, you'll see how your entire viewpoint will shift and you'll move forward quickly.

Consider the questions below and see if you can spot areas in your life where you've been reluctant to change. Write down the answers that might be worth exploring further.

- What previous failures are still holding you back?

- Have you tried to improve the efficiency of your business but failed because you didn't know how?

- What inefficiencies have you tolerated because you felt there was no way to fix them?

- What fears and areas of reluctance do you need to overcome?

You may be responding to your past. You may not even be aware that those old patterns are affecting your decisions. It is *critical* that you don't allow fear to stop you from implementing the powerful proven strategies you'll discover in this book. If you persist, if you *push through*, you can change your old patterns and succeed.

Remember that no one ever succeeds by conforming to the norm. You succeed when you adjust your environment to suit your needs. Did Steve Jobs conform to his environment? Did Bill Gates allow the resistance of IBM's "ruling class" to stop him?

Trust me, by following the specific suggestions in this book and those on my website (all of which are designed to help you sidestep the problems most early adapters have), a transition will be a lot easier for you. If you are reluctant, keep reading with an open mind. The benefits are worth the effort.

Myth #2: I'll lose control of my company.

Instead of losing control of your organization, the opposite will happen. By tracking your staff and your sales processes more precisely than before, you will be able to react faster to situations as they arise and respond quickly and appropriately. Your systems will show you anomalies in productivity flow, sales trends, and manufacturing very quickly.

Most CEOs who start down this road are cautious at the beginning, but they soon see progress as one division after another successfully bridges their remote work force back to the rest of the company. It is inspiring to watch as the first team is sent home, only to come back online ready to go using their new cloud-based systems. Usually within the first year, as overhead expenses subside and profits improve, the management team accelerates the progress of completing the transition.

In chapter five, I explain more about the systems in question and how they will make this possible.

Myth #3: I can't transition now. I've just invested a fortune.

The money you've invested in capital equipment will fully depreciate over the next five to seven years. Are you going to stay stuck with those systems instead of moving forward? As you probably have a continuous upgrade/replacement cycle like most companies, it may seem that the timing is never right. Don't buy into the myth.

As most internal server-based software systems are migrated to the cloud, the excess hardware can be sold to recover capital. Most of your budgeted capital equipment expenses will drop to the bottom line as much less is required than before. And even though your monthly subscription fees for cloud-based systems will increase, compared to the expenses shed, there really is no contest. Your expenses will be reduced significantly, especially since monthly service fees are based on usage while the systems you actually do use will constantly be upgraded and maintained by those providing your services.

While some of your IT staff might become redundant, you will still need IT staff who know how to customize your new software environment.

The right time is now. Start to plan the proper execution of your conversion, and learn to master the management skills required to lead your team.

Myth #4: My company is doing fine. There is no need to transition.

It is great that your company is doing well today, but the world is changing. If you don't adapt you will be left behind, and you may not do as well in the near future. It is time to make the transition to a far more powerful environment, an environment that saves money and improves the service level you provide to your clients across every business unit.

The transition is now easier than ever before. Cloud-based systems vendors are more than happy to help you. No matter how well your company is performing at the moment, moving to a completely Invisible Organization is the most efficient, obvious path to continue your progress and growth.

Myth #5: My IT people have looked at the cloud systems, and we are all set.

If your IT department tells you that you have the latest and greatest systems, you may want to check with other CEOs who have been through this experience with their own companies.

Ask questions and do some research on your own. Take one of your best IT guys and tell him you need him to help you create Version 2.0 of your organization by helping you move to a virtual environment. Ensure him of your trust, and emphasize your need for visionary IT executives. This way your IT staff will understand that they are part of the future of your organization, and they won't feel threatened by the transition. Create advocates by sharing the vision.

Myth #6: It can't be done with my current resources.

Most of us are working with limited funding and staff as it is, so this thought is understandable. But in reality, resources are far less important than you think. It's really more about getting buy-in from your management team and IT staff, then organizing your data and work flow so the rest of your team can easily and quickly perform their jobs. That way management can monitor and track the progress of all tasks and client assignments. Your organization beforehand is much more important to your success and the growth of your company than your resources.

The challenge is not the technology. The skills of the CEO dictate if the transition will be rapid or slow, whether the company will succeed or fail in going invisible. That is why you have to make sure your management skills are up to the task.

Running and managing a virtual work force is very different than managing a traditional company. When your organization is invisible, you can't walk around and check in with people, observe how they are dressed or take note of what time they show up for work and depart. Instead you are monitoring more important elements of productivity and client interactions. That is why in a virtual environment you need to be even more concerned with your people.

Your personal and management skills, the way you communicate with others, the enthusiasm you generate, and your pride in "the mission" will all determine your success as an invisible CEO. Your patience and your skills will be tested to the limit with a virtual team. Honing these skills before your conversion will make everything go faster. As you continue reading this book, you'll learn how to determine who fits in best in your invisible team.

Myth #7: There is no way my staff will cooperate.

This is simply not true. Your staff will cooperate if you lay out in advance exactly what will happen, when it will happen, and how it will affect each and every person in the organization. When the benefits of working from home are fully understood, no one will object—the freedom of having more control over their schedules will far outweigh their fears or concerns. When everyone fully understands that there is a well-thought-out plan and there will be benefits for the staff, as well as the company and the clients, enthusiasm will build as the team starts the transitioning process.

The key ingredients to make your staff successful

No one likes to be taken for granted. Everyone wants to be respected, no matter where they are on the org chart. Even if there is no org chart, treating people with respect and having high expectations actually changes the way your staff see themselves. That is why leadership and communication skills are the most critical tools you will need to build your Invisible Organization.

Unfortunately, as CEOs most of us were not trained to build our staff up effectively and to bring out the best in them, unless you were one of the lucky ones who had a great mentor to help you develop the leadership skills needed to run a large organization. I was lucky. I was already an excellent communicator, and more recently, I had Chet Holmes and Tony Robbins as my mentors.

Applying the management techniques I'm sharing with you can transform how your staff members behave and increase their enthusiasm for the changes you are about to make. If you are skillful in bringing this transition about, the results you seek will happen quickly and with as little confusion as possible. Then, as you encourage your team to develop their own skills, everyone will contribute on a much higher level.

Once you have your new systems in place, you can manage actual productivity. Suddenly it's no longer relevant how long it takes someone to get coffee or attend to other common workday interruptions. Personal habits are now monitored electronically. Your job is to set up exception reports to see what isn't getting done as planned.

What counts is:

✓ How happy are your staff members?

✓ How happy are your clients?

✓ How well is your staff serving your clients?

In an Invisible Organization, it's even more important to recognize the value of every single person in the company. *The heightened value of enhanced communication cannot be overstressed* since people want to feel connected—to the leadership and to each other.

The most powerful CEOs are the best communicators. That requires more than just sending an email or recording a video on your phone. Using the assessment I've provided, you will know how to measure what is most important to you and your staff when it comes to enjoying work, being productive and creating a great culture inside your Invisible Organization. Go to www.InvisibleOrganization.com/Resources to take a test that will help you assess your staff's values.

Five tips to improve your staff performance:

1. Recognize individual contributions.

Your people are valuable! Even your lowest level staff members work for you because you chose them. Treat those staff members with respect and acknowledge them regularly. Make them feel valuable by thanking them for their service and giving them meaningful updates. Go out of your way to plan communication with every level of your staff. Teach your management to do the same and stress the importance of doing so. Pay your staff well. Following this model, you can pay a premium to the market for talent and still reap higher profits.

2. Profit share with every staff member.

The percentage may be miniscule, but the impact is massive. Find a way to make *all* staff feel like owners. A tiny percentage of profit sharing gives most staff members a totally different perspective on how they should treat clients, how long they want to stay with the company, and who they are really working for. Meaning: their compensation is now partially dependent on the customer's experience. If the customer's experience stinks, their pay will suffer for it.

Paying for a higher level of performance will heavily enhance both the dedication of your staff and your customers' experience. This is often called *incentive pay*.

Note: The word "bonus" has lost its effectiveness as it has been used so much. When you tell your staff they will share in the profits of the company, it becomes more meaningful to them.

3. **Make all job training a qualification to be employed.**

If a new hire can't pass a test at an acceptable level, he can't have the job. This way you'll immediately know how qualified your workforce is. Match those best qualified with the most demanding jobs. The rest will learn to work harder to find and keep employment. It also is the purest form of the merit system. As people become more skilled, they can apply for better or higher paying jobs inside the company.

4. **Make client testimonials a goal that results in individual and team rewards for exceptional service.**

Give your staff a reason to go above and beyond. Your clients will learn to expect great service from you, and your workforce will be eager to bend over backwards to get that next testimonial. Make this a point of pride. You could even construct a contest for the number of testimonials obtained for great service.

5. **Create an environment where the staff can grow with the company as long as the company keeps growing.**

Explain in advance that people must get better at their jobs and must earn promotions in order to remain with the company. Also, make it clear that nobody will be promoted in any pre-set amount of time. If someone is not adding enough value to the company or has outgrown his current job, he may be asked to leave. There's no sense in paying people who aren't invested in helping you grow. You don't want people in your company who are just looking for a paycheck.

You are in business to make clients happy, and everything your staff members do should reflect that. You want raving fans, or "ambassadors," as I call my best clients. That may sound impossible, but it can be an everyday occurrence in a company that respects its staff and shows it actively. Happy staff members feel they are part of a company that has a purpose and means something to this world. They will take ownership, because they are part of a movement bigger than themselves where their contribution, no matter how small on the surface it may appear, is critical to the company's success. Be that company, build that company, thrill your staff, and you will be unstoppable.

Your vision, your WHY, drives your organization. Revisit the reasons why you created your company in the first place, and then share this with your team. When everyone is on board with your mission, your staff will be motivated by a higher purpose than just a paycheck or a sale.

Myth #8: I can't train my staff properly if they aren't onsite.

Weeks of training can be required to bring a new staff member to the point where he can speak confidently with a prospect and is familiar with the systems. It requires well-crafted training systems to track each candidate through the maze of training requirements and results. It also takes measurement systems to see how quickly staff learn and then deploy their skills.

Virtual systems enable you to do this. In the case of client interaction, most companies record their phone calls. These recordings become the basis for many of the most productive training sessions available to newly hired staff.

I have yet to see a company using a well-designed interactive and automated training system fail to produce quality staff members faster and with less management time.

Myth #9: How the heck will I hire quality people without even meeting them?

It's easy to see how people can abuse the privilege of working from home. That's why it's important to know how to screen and hire them without ever meeting them face-to-face. At Business Breakthroughs International, we had several different teams of top producers all working from home. Their work ethic was visible in "weekly stats" that showed all elements of their productivity.

There are probably a hundred people who identify themselves for any given job and who might have some experience. But ultimately, do they have the characteristics that have made *your company* successful? If not, then they may not be a good match, and they'll only end up costing you time and money. You need to know how to avoid a bad hire, especially in a key position.

If you take these few pages and send them to H/R along with your hiring managers, you should see a jump in the quality of your new hires. Put simply, you need to look beyond the resume and evaluate a person's psychological profile. Your time, money, and energy should be invested <u>only</u> in those most likely to thrive in *your* organization!

Note: I have arranged with a preferred vendor, whom we have used for years, to get you the best personality testing assessments possible at a very big discount. Please go to <u>www.InvisibleOrganization.com/Resources</u> to access the vendor and the discount code.

It's true that negative people can secretly thrive in an Invisible Organization if no one is looking for them. They spread resentment more easily with less attention and can destroy your organization from the inside out. Fortunately, there is a "sniff test" to help you tell if someone is going to work out: you need to screen for *life disposition.*

Life disposition describes how happy and cheerful a person really is. If you want your staff to be positive and upbeat and to look and act professionally, then they need to have a good life disposition. You can quickly and simply spot how one views life. When you talk to a person, is he or she looking down or in your eyes? Even if you never meet your prospective staff member face-to-face, trust your feelings. You can get a really good sense over the phone or on Skype.

A simple way to discover someone's life disposition during an interview is to ask about the "peak experiences" in his or her life. Don't make a suggestion of positives or negatives, just watch and see how the person responds naturally.

If he mentions that he has faced a lot of setbacks, you get an indication of his way of thinking. If, on the other hand, he talks about moments of triumph, things in life he's proud of, it's a good sign. That's the kind of person you want to hire, given that everything else about him is a fit. Over time you'll notice that discerning someone's life disposition becomes second nature to you. When you truly master a skill, you can use it without having to think about it.

However, just because a person seems to have a positive life disposition doesn't necessarily mean that he's the right fit. Sometimes they are deceiving you because they think they know what you are looking for. They are wrong because even if they do get through, your personality test phase will likely spot those who fake it. Even if they get through the screening process, they won't last long in an organization where most everyone else is really upbeat and positive.

Sometimes the timing can be off. Of course, everybody goes through ups and downs in life. It's just not a good idea to hire someone when he's going through difficulties.

In 2002 after my divorce, I felt so devastated that I was basically worthless as an executive for a solid year. I had such a sense of failure that I couldn't enjoy life. I lost interest in many things, including my most passionate pursuit, photography, which I have immersed myself in since the 70's. However, once I bounced back and changed my life disposition, good things started to come my way again.

The real question is, *"What is your life disposition?"* Are you a happy person? Who you are will determine whether or not you're likely to attract others who have a happy life disposition. After all, staff often mirrors the "boss." So it's best to be upbeat, positive, confident, and appreciative of the people around you.

Once you have busted the myths and overcome any resistance or doubts, you will be able to determine the value of going invisible. Even marginal use of the strategies in this book will produce a significantly more productive staff and could contribute to an increase in profits within the first few months. When *you* take the initiative to make it happen, expand your skills, build your team and set up your systems, your company *can* become invisible with your current resources—and you will enjoy the many benefits. But it all starts with you. You may be delighted to discover that it's actually easier than you think.

3

Realities That Enable
You to Go Invisible

Just imagine how much fun it will be to run your Invisible Organization from the deck of your yacht, the patio of your oceanfront villa, or your own 45-foot motorhome traveling the country and enjoying life.

When I worked for Tony and Chet, I worked at the location of my choice every day: in hotel rooms, on a sailboat, on a plane, and even from several foreign countries. Once I was in Tuscany on one of my many photo trips around the world. Looking out of my window I watched the beautiful colors of the sunset with my MacBook open running Skype and taking care of business. Earlier that day I had spent a couple of hours on team management calls and had approved the new marketing campaigns.

Whether you'll succeed in creating this lifestyle as an invisible CEO depends on you and your ability as a leader. There are hundreds of management books about how to become a better executive. Even though many are valuable, I will give you a new perspective on the qualities you'll need when you embark on the journey of building and running your Invisible Organization. They have proven to get results—for me and for my clients.

Reality #1: It Requires Specific Leadership Skills to Run an Invisible Organization.

The stronger your leadership and the clearer your vision, the more aligned your staff will be. In the thirty-five years that I've led my own teams, I've worked with some of the best... and worst leaders. Without great leadership, teams suffer, profits sink and clients leave. Mastering leadership skills is not hard, but it is crucial.

Management flaws and lack of leadership skills will become even more evident in an Invisible Organization. That is why it's important to know the key components you'll need to improve your own leadership as well as that of your management team.

Clients will ultimately see the animation of your vision in every single encounter. Poor leadership and a lack of vision, on the other hand, will leave your staff feeling unsettled. That is why it's critically important that you focus on yourself first. You'll need to master specific skills to lead your Invisible Organization successfully.

A full leadership assessment is available on www. InvisibleOrganization.com/Resources. By working through the assessment, you will be able to pinpoint areas you'll need to improve in order to succeed as an invisible CEO.

Reality #2: Weaknesses Are Magnified, but So Are Strengths.

When you run an Invisible Organization, every action will be even more significant since you will work remotely most of the time. You might have been able to get away with sloppy behavior or poor communications skills in the past, but with an invisible workforce, poor communication skills will cause big problems.

Once you master the specific skills needed to lead your Invisible Organization, your team will love and respect you. You will generate rock-solid loyalty from your team—and from your clients. If you are wondering how, here is the breakdown of the individual skills and traits that you and your staff need to succeed.

Have a Clear Vision — The ability to see the future regardless of what others tell you will give you the conviction to succeed. In order to accomplish any great feat, you *must* have the end goal in mind. Past failures, critics, and people who'll resist you because they are scared of change, won't be able to stop you. Visualize your Invisible Organization in your mind, imagine what it will *feel like*, and know that you *will* realize it. A clear vision can be collaborative and a work-in-progress. By involving your management team, you will create loyalty and trust; you will teach them "best practices," which is incredibly motivating. Train them to do the same with their staff.

• What is your vision for your company?

Be Motivated by Passion — There *will* be obstacles on the path to great achievement, and creating an Invisible Organization will be no exception. You need passion to be able to execute in the face of unending hurdles. This is one of the most important ingredients needed to lead your team. Your clients and your staff will know if your passion is genuine. The stronger it is, the easier it will be to inspire others to follow you. Passion shows up when it's needed most. In the face of hardship and challenges, your passion for winning and for serving your clients must shine through. Show your strength and dedication to the company and to the team by showing up strong—your enthusiasm, sense of humor, and clarity of vision make you a leader.

Focus on Your Mission — Your mission is what drives everyone forward in a unified voice. If you are the founder, you had a goal when you first set out to build your business. If you truly believe, for example, that your clients deserve to be served at the highest level, then that's your mission. No matter what industry you are in, your mission is to deliver and serve the best possible experience to your clients.

• Are you passionate about your mission?

• Can you communicate your mission clearly to others?

Build Strong Credibility — Credibility goes hand-in-hand with confidence. You must know what you're talking about and be convincing. If you can quickly and directly show the value of your offer before a group of investors or clients, you'll be able to make the sale. Your integrity, experience, and *credibility* play a huge role in attracting teammates, investors, and clients. Credibility really means having a track record of being that guy who gets it done no matter what. If you do so honestly and with integrity, your credibility will soar.

- Can you define why you are credible enough for clients to trust you?

- What could you do to increase your credibility?

Be Honest — Honesty is possibly the most important human trait in personal and professional relationships. It's extremely important to be *honest* with yourself. For me, being honest with myself means not making excuses for bad behavior—mine or anyone else's. This also means that I make decisions based on a clear, honest assessment of any given situation. My management team knows this, and even though they may not like my decisions, they respect my honesty. I expect my management team, as well as the other staff, to honestly weigh all known facts before they make decisions. Whether your staff is virtual or not, they will notice this and conclude that your company is run by a team of people who are clear about their values.

I once had a boss who was an alcoholic, but he would never admit to it. Since he couldn't be honest with himself, he couldn't honestly assess others. One day one of his salesmen got arrested for drunk driving with a client in the car. When my boss heard about it, he laughingly congratulated the salesman for not losing the order. The next day the buyer's boss read what had happened in the newspaper, and the company lost the account. My boss's bad decisions made some good people leave. This is an extreme situation, yet it demonstrates that being able to be honest with yourself and others is one of the key determining factors to personal and corporate success.

Your staff is investing their time and life in your business. Give them a reason to operate every day in a way that will make them feel proud of what they do. If you are honest with your staff, they will chew through walls for you. Honesty is a powerful tool, especially in the face of challenging conditions, because it inspires *trust*.

• Can you be direct and forthright with your team even when you have bad news to deliver? Or do you sugarcoat the truth and spin it instead?

• Have you helped your team feel safe in an environment of honesty?

Be Trustworthy — Trust goes hand in hand with honesty. If you are honest consistently, you will earn the trust of others. Trust is an important factor in making decisions quickly. An excellent book on the subject is The Speed of Trust by Steven M.R. Covey. I strongly recommend reading this book, because it provides specific strategies and techniques for building trust as well as rebuilding trust if it has been broken. It also explains how building trust can be converted to "relationship equity." When someone can be trusted, no contracts or lawyers are required, just a strong handshake and the deal is done, the work started, the investment made. Afterwards, you can paper the deal so no one forgets the agreement details. Since your staff, clients and vendors may be thousands of miles away and you won't often meet with them in person, trust is crucial for the success of every Invisible Organization.

- Can you effectively determine who in your organization deserves your unqualified and complete trust and who doesn't?

- Are you known to be trustworthy?

Follow a Solid Strategy — Vision and a sound strategy will get you to the finish line. Craft your strategy, shape it, and plan for possible upsets. A tricky obstacle here is not to get so bogged down in planning that you never take action. Imperfect action and follow-through will always be superior to a perfect plan that never gets executed. There are dozens of books written about business strategy. Study the work of some of the greatest business minds that have invented great strategies such as Jay Abraham and Peter Drucker.

- Do you have a solid strategy?

- How much time do you spend with your team coaching them to help execute your strategy?

- Do your failed strategies get as much attention and review as your successful ones?

Have Empathy — Empathy is the key to *establishing strong bonds* with your employees, co-workers and clients because it leads to affinity. An individual who is warm and insightful will build stronger relationships than someone who takes a strictly intellectual approach. Focus on the other person and not on yourself. Make an effort to truly understand the person you are talking to and be *genuinely* interested in making a connection. Approach relationships with the mindset that *every* person has something to offer in terms of human experience. Knowing this, you'll open up and your humanity will shine through.

- How well do you know your staff?

- Does your staff know you?

- What could you do on a daily or weekly basis to improve your relationship with your staff and your clients?

Master Communication Skills — Very few people understand the components of real communication. Listening is an art. You must establish a common *reality* first to communicate successfully and build a relationship. People find common interests in sports, hobbies, foods, movies, or work.

Here is a great example:

At a business mastermind with a group of high-level experts in their fields (most of them charging about $20,000 per day), everyone was asked to share something personal. When we began to share our deepest darkest secrets, something amazing happened. *Poof!* The big ego balloons popped. The facades melted, and all of a sudden we connected deeply as friends as well as business associates. The truth was that everyone had failed miserably in almost every aspect of their lives at one time or another. Yet, using our skills and abilities, we had also fought back relentlessly to achieve the success we now have.

Remember, this was a room filled with very successful business leaders. Many were multi-millionaires, and some were very well known. Yet one of us had been a drug addict, another had been involved in organized crime, another had been an international smuggler, and yet another had spent time in prison.

Nobody had led a perfect life. We all had made some bad mistakes. We had suffered the defeats of failure, but in the end we had gotten over it, picked ourselves up and continued on with life. That's how we all had found success.

Once we shared the common reality of the challenges we had faced, we felt empathy. We bonded, and that bond opened the door for real communication.

- What can you do to make the other person feel truly heard?

- How can you make sure that your message will be received?

Demonstrate Executive Mettle — Mettle is your ability to cope with difficulties or to face a demanding situation in a resilient way. It will help you turn your vision into reality, despite the doubters and critics. Mettle comes from your passion about your vision of the future for your company and products, and it will allow you to crystalize your determination into focused effort. All businesses go through phases of difficulty. Some CEOs fight for their lives (as in a legal battle), while others choose to give up.

Executive mettle means standing up to your Board of Directors when you are sure you are right and proving to them that your conviction is based on sound strategy backed up by your management team. This quality develops through experience by leading teams to successful outcomes.

The strength of your vision, your passion, and your conviction will hold your team together. But without empathy, communication skills, honesty and trust, you may temporarily get what you want, but you'll rarely be truly successful. When you master the skills mentioned above you'll be an extraordinary leader, especially if you have developed the advanced skill of building consensus.

It is a very powerful and important skill, because no leader gets very far without learning how to build consensus among peers and teams and developing the finesse to employ them carefully and artfully. New leaders don't do that very well in general, while some leaders can do it naturally with a head nod. An experienced leader works behind the scenes to sell his project to his team before the big meeting, the big presentation or the board meeting by clearly and directly communicating with each person one-on-one, answering questions and dealing with their objections. They feel respected, because they have been given a chance to have their say. Later when new plans are announced, there will be no surprises. Everyone has already bought into the vision and knows where they stand. That's true consensus building.

To print out the entire list above, including more robust discussions about each of the specific leadership skills required, go to www.InvisibleOrganization.com/Resources.

Reality #3: It Can Get Lonely at the Top.

Sometimes it can get lonely and stressful at the top. Having owned and run several companies myself, I know what it's like when everyone turns to you for answers and you wish you had somebody *you* could talk to. Or you have a great idea for your company and you want somebody to bounce it off of, but your management team lacks the bigger picture to give you the input you are looking for.

This is why there are CEO mastermind groups, coaches and advisors, all of which can help you lead with a fresh perspective. CEOs need support and counsel, too. If you are interested in communicating with a group of like-minded individuals, you can consider a mastermind for CEOs who run virtual companies of all types at www.InvisibleOrganization.com/Resources.

Reality #4: When You Spot a Problem, You've Got to Take Action Quickly!

It may sound surprising, but in an Invisible Organization you'll notice when something isn't right much sooner, because you'll be tracking productivity and results carefully and you'll see tiny changes in statistics quickly. As long as you communicate actively, your staff will understand that you care, but won't tolerate a slip in performance. Spotting problems right away before they get out of hand is far more efficient. It's more caring to take action immediately than to wait for a staff member to fail. By acting as a leader, your management and staff will know what they can expect. Without clear guidelines no one is comfortable.

Imagine that you hear from your VP Marketing that your ad agency screwed up and placed the wrong ad. You are out $25,000 and have lost a month of promotion. Clearly the VP wasn't watching the agency carefully enough. Best to fire that person, right? If you do so before attempting to help your executive with the problem, you are telegraphing to the rest of your staff that they are next if they expose a problem. By creating an ambiance where management and staff feel safe and comfortable instead, they are more likely to bring problems to your attention.

This is all about helping good people develop trust in your vision, your leadership and your experience. Some of the best people make bad mistakes sometimes and as long as it wasn't due to gross negligence or ill intentions, consider giving that person a second chance. Another viewpoint to consider is that you just paid $25,000 to educate your VP Marketing that mistakes like that can wreck a productive quarter and destroy a nearly perfect career. You paid the price anyway, you might as well get the benefits of a very well trained VP who will likely NEVER make that mistake again!

Being Challenged Doesn't Mean You Get to Screw Up

Don't allow personal challenges to interfere or cloud your judgment, as this will negatively impact the company. When you're willing to confront the problem or the person with the problem, you can work towards solutions.

Here's an example: I once knew an entrepreneur who had an amazing career. He was a self-starter with a number of successful businesses under his belt, even during childhood. As a seasoned head of business, he led an Internet company to millions of dollars in profits. Then, without warning, things suddenly went sour. Sales dropped. Management turned on him. And investors lost their confidence in him.

The young CEO was going to be out of a job and possibly ruined if he couldn't turn things around quickly. Everyone else had noticed the changes in his behavior except for him—he was too wrapped up in his personal problems to see what was happening. He didn't realize how bad things had become, and it came down to a meeting with his board of directors.

He decided to be honest and upfront with his board and management team. He explained that he was dealing with huge personal challenges, and the stress was more than distracting. His alcoholic wife was endangering their infant child, she was involved with another man, and she was running up huge secret credit card accounts. He offered to resign, but the board gave him thirty days to turn the company around. Privately, board members confessed that they, too, had been dealing with alcoholic spouses or had done so in the past. We are all people, and a little humanity at the right moment can change the direction of what may seem to be hard and fast decisions.

Can you imagine having that going on in your life while trying to run an Internet startup? Being a true leader, though, he mustered the confidence and refocused all his energy on fixing everything that was wrong with the company. Not only did he fix the problems, but he found a way to sell the company at the same time.

Unfortunately, we all have problems that may interfere with our performance from time to time, but a true executive needs to be aware of the affect he's having on the company.

Or maybe you've had a similar experience where a staff member seemed to have lost his mojo. Others might not have noticed the lack of enthusiasm, the appointments missed, or the balls dropped that caused the company to lose a big client. The reason isn't always obvious.

Reality #5: Building Management Skills Is an Ongoing Effort.

Your company will flourish if you know exactly how to develop the right skills in your management team. By spotting potential issues early, you'll create a work environment where your staff can thrive. Once you and your management team are able to recognize what is going on, then the issues can be fixed with care and attention.

Let's see if you recognize any of these symptoms in yourself or your management team:

• Entrepreneur's disease

This is the inability to delegate. Even non-entrepreneurs can suffer from it. Maybe you think you can manage your tasks faster and better than anyone else. Or you were a great salesman who was promoted to management, but then you failed to lead your team because you couldn't step out of your old role. What is the cure? Realize that you don't want to be a solo-preneur. Your company can only be successful if you train and trust others. The same is true for your staff—you need to help them see that delegating will aid their advancement and their income.

- Being stuck

A division is in a slump. You've tried lots of different strategies, but you just can't figure it out. Even though you're smart, capable and experienced, that doesn't mean that you'll always know the next step. As the CEO, you will need a "secret" advisor. Seek out a CEO mentor and *use* that person to keep you on track. Encourage your staff to ask for help, and make sure they know you appreciate them when they do.

- Loss of trust

Sometimes teams lose trust in their leader. This *does* happen, but it *can* be fixed. You just have to be willing to explore the reasons why your team has lost trust in you or a manager. Then you must be willing to rebuild that trust. It starts with being honest about why trust was lost. An honest conversation goes a long way to clearing the air and setting the stage for that second chance. Lost trust is fixed by excessive honesty for prolonged periods of time.

- Loss of interest

Sometimes people just stop caring. If you could hear what goes on inside another person's mind, it might sound like this: "If I can hold out a little longer, I'll unload my shares and I can move on."

You should take this as a wake-up call. You need to fix this dangerous condition quickly. One of your managers or Vice

Presidents can lose interest as well. If you have good people working for him or her, they will probably spot this before you do. In a compassionate, performance-driven organization, people will speak up and let you know because they care. What are the signs of disinterest? When a person is not as focused as he used to be, it's time to ask questions. Never let someone else's agenda interfere with your plans to grow the company. Keep in mind that a senior staff member who has lost interest may be subconsciously interested in failing so he can be relieved of his duties.

• Inability to cope

Stress is a reality of leadership. When stressed, leaders have a tendency to ignore the warning signs and tell themselves that they can handle it. Stress needs to be dealt with honestly because it can lead to poor decision-making. It affects happiness, quality of life, and health. While stress is a part of the job, it's also manageable. You need to be willing to heed the warning signs that someone is in trouble and help them learn how to minimize the stress in their life.

What is stress? Stress is created when someone believes they are under financial or time pressure, and they don't believe there is a solution to the problem. Whether there is a solution or not, worrying doesn't solve the problem. Instead, focus on creative possibilities that can improve the situation. Great solutions may become hidden during peak stress periods. Our job as CEOs is to prevent unnecessary stress in our most precious staff members: the management team. *Acceptance after action* is the most powerful way of handling stress. The CEO needs to acknowledge when a staff member screws up and then, after the lesson is learned, let it go. Well-designed and implemented systems are a great way to avoid stress, because they reduce the number of variables that can go wrong and expose problems early.

Reality #6: All Problems Can be Fixed—or They Solve Themselves.

If you don't solve a problem as soon as possible, the problem may resolve in a way you don't like. Why not have a process for all types of problems so they can be solved quickly and easily?

It's best to have a checklist with "tools" that can expedite finding the solution. Disseminate them throughout your organization, and you'll keep your company functioning at the highest level.

• Listen

As the CEO, you will know when your company is suffering from lack of trust. Generally it's a lack of trust of the leadership. Simply listen to staff and hear them out in a non-judgmental way. Sit down one-on-one with each member of your team and have an open conversation. Let them know you're not going to sit by and let things get worse. This sets the stage for direct, serious communication. *Really listen* to what they have to say. Don't react. Allow them to express themselves, how they feel, what they see about the company that you're unable to see. Look for a few characteristics during your conversation:

- o Are they feeling negative about the company?
- o Are they feeling negative about you?
- o Is there conflict between team members?

Show how you listen nonjudgmentally and then encourage your management team to do the same. If they understand how you do it, they will do it, too.

- Get the reasons why

Learn as much as you can about the issue raised. Listen carefully and try to decipher if those involved are protecting themselves by blaming someone else. Ask open questions about their experiences and their feelings about the team. Get complete answers. Thank them and move on to the next person. Don't stop until you've heard from everyone on the (executive) team.

- The Third Party Rule

Whenever there's conflict between two people, a third party is almost always the culprit. Someone is whispering in the ear of one of the conflicted parties. Until you find the third party who's responsible, you won't be able to resolve the conflict. The hidden third party will continue to interfere. Dig deep and find the culprit. It's vital that you cut out this cancer and move on.

This concept is so important that I would say emphatically that most conflicts are caused by third parties.

This could be someone willfully sabotaging orders, parts or inventory and letting someone else take the blame. When that person is berated for doing a poor job, the third party is almost always present to enjoy the show. Look carefully. They are usually lurking in the background physically or otherwise. Some are very clever, making it nearly impossible to detect them unless you are aware of this kind of situation.

- Expand your resources

Most entrepreneurs run their small businesses in a frenzy of activity, trying to do everything themselves. Instead of figuring things out by yourself, build a support network around you and take advantage of the many resources available to you.

✓ Set up a board of advisors. Offer them shares in the company to keep them engaged.

✓ Build a relationship with your bank even if you have investors.

✓ Join a mastermind group of like-minded individuals.

✓ Find a coach or consultant who has been in your shoes and who has achieved success. Having someone with experience in your corner will greatly increase the odds of your success.

✓ Consider a business partner who complements you and has the same level of commitment. (It doesn't have to be a 50/50 split.)

✓ Encourage your management team to keep learning, join a mastermind, and attend events and seminars. They will perform better with peer review and support. Ask for feedback on how this is working out for your team.

✓ Learn to delegate and teach others to delegate

You are responsible for the well-being of the company. That does *not* mean you have to do everything yourself. Remember, the most valuable commodity of your business is the management of time. You therefore want to compartmentalize anything and everything that *doesn't* require your personal attention. Make sure your management team understands how valuable their time is to the company. Encourage them to use the resources they have instead of wasting their own time.

• Keep learning

Read books or listen to audio books. Never stop developing your craft. You can get a *great* education from the super-successful when you buy their training programs or attend their seminars. You can learn how to handle stress, improve your communication skills, and deal better with life's challenges. Build a library of skill-based training courses and make them available from the cloud so your management team understands that constantly learning is the only way to advance in your organization.

Reality #7: Creating a Strong Company Culture May be Harder, but It Can Be Done!

If your company operates more with electrons (computers, software, video) rather than atoms (buildings, desks, parking lots, etc.), you can't walk around and drop by someone's office. It's obviously not possible to meet with others in person if they are spread over different states, maybe even different continents.

Encourage multiple means of communication within and between teams. There are simple tools like HipChat.com that allow people to set up virtual rooms for group conversations where they come and go throughout the day. A more sophisticated and useful tool to accomplish group communication is Moxtra.com which creates a common set of to-do's, documents and group chat so that teams can manage specific issues quickly and easily. If you go to the resource center on www.InvisibleOrganization.com, you will find a link to a free account.

Use tools that encourage greater, closer communications, and everyone will enjoy the interaction and be thankful it exists. This is all part of keeping people connected so they can be closer and united in the vision of the company to deliver a superior experience to clients.

By finding a bigger purpose that your people resonate with, a purpose that is meaningful to them and not just to the company, you will bond your team to a common mission. When your company culture permeates your organization, everyone is well-trained, and the staff know what the company does and what its mission is. Your automated training systems insure that everyone knows how to solve problems, deal with clients, and leave those clients feeling like they want to tell others about their experience. Clients and new staff members will notice there is something uniquely different about your company.

Once you have great people working for your company, you want to keep them motivated, excited and happy. The key to productive staff is paying attention to their needs, having open communication, and paying them an excellent wage based on their performance. (In chapter 10 I'll cover how to hire Sales Superstars for your Invisible Organization.)

By getting behind a charitable cause, you'll create purpose for people beyond their usual company work. Survey your team and find a charity that everyone believes in. Set aside a tiny amount (percentage-wise) to contribute to this charity or give your staff permission to volunteer on paid workdays. I've seen how these strategies can help to unify a team. My employees were proud that their hard work also helped others.

In my last company, VP Sales Rosina Fischer did this with great success, even donating her own money to back up her conviction. She set sales records with this simple technique. She motivated people by fostering the belief that business is as much about contributing to the community as it is about making a profit for the shareholders.

Progressive companies like Zappos actually pay thousands of dollars for newly hired staff to quit if they don't fit in the culture. They want their employees to love their jobs. They don't want people to work for them because they need the money but because they enjoy doing what their job requires. If someone would rather have $6,000 than his job with Zappos, he doesn't belong in the company.

That's how important culture is.

Culture is nothing more than how it feels to work inside an organization. If the life disposition of an individual is upbeat, happy and enthusiastically oriented to helping people, then they probably fit in your culture.

In an Invisible Organization, there are many different ways to keep the environment exciting and interesting. For example, you could start a contest that gets your staff involved in finding new team members, identifying new markets, or coming up with creative advertising ideas. You can ignite a healthy competitive spirit by rewarding the person who comes up with the best ideas. The goal is to find anything that you can use to rally the company around a common goal.

Imagine if one person in your company was responsible on creating a weekly profile on someone who works there. Their job, would be to create a profile showing this person's hobbies, passions, accomplishments and qualities beyond the work they produce. Imagine the way it might feel when one-at-a-time, each staff member is profiled in the most positive light and then publicized inside the company. How special would someone feel? How many new friends might they make? What would that do for morale? Get the picture?

****

A Personal Story about a Winner's Mentality

Many of us have memories of times in our lives when we felt on top of the world. Well, one of the greatest times in my life was back in the 1990s. After having built a very successful company, we reaped the rewards for a number of years. Timeslips Corp. was a company that published software to help service professionals bill by the hour. We not only met a need within the market with our innovative software, we created a high quality product.

As a result of creating a great product, we won "The Best Software Award" in our category for five consecutive years. What an amazing accomplishment! But then suddenly, totally unexpectedly, we went from being praised and honored as one of the best in the industry to struggling to keep our clients.

It turned out that there were bugs in our software that we didn't catch before making the product available for purchase that particular year. This major error put our company in a real bind. Customers were angry, and morale among employees was the lowest ever. People were pointing fingers and blaming each other. More than anything, psychologically, everyone was questioning and second-guessing themselves.

We had our first bad product review in history. We had an increase in tech support calls, and the chatter in CompuServe forums was getting negative. On top of that, we were late with our next upgrade and still missing some badly needed features. We could have totally fallen apart as a company— but we didn't.

How did this terrible mistake happen? We didn't do enough quality testing. We never found out why the bug in the software wasn't detected early on, but we had to recover, fix the problem, and regain our reputation.

We first apologized to our clients for a poor showing. We suspended all tech support contracts and fixed everyone's problems for free. We did our best to go above and beyond by Fed-Exing discs out (Internet downloads weren't available back then), and we even sent paid consultants to our client offices to fix serious issues.

People are quick to assume that a downfall is due to an individual or organization getting comfortable and taking their success for granted. That wasn't the case in our situation. The reality is that adversity is part of life. What do you do when adversity comes? How do you respond when you experience defeat and your "winner's mentality" is tested?

I was desperately searching for a way to get the company back on track. As a leader, I was trying my best to keep a positive attitude so that I could help employees do the same. Trying to remain upbeat myself, I was doing a lot of soul-searching looking for answers and inspiration.

I found that inspiration by focusing on the solution and knowing that we could and would recover our dignity and our standing in the marketplace.

Timeslips Corp. rebounded from one poor year in which a faulty product was sold to our customers after years of excellence. As a strong team with a "winning attitude," we didn't allow ourselves to stay down for long. We focused on solving the problem, rolled up our sleeves, and did whatever it took to experience our previous level of success.

The following year we were back on top, winning "The Best Software of the Year Award" yet again, and we continued to win during all the years I ran that company.

One of my greatest blessings came in the form of my daughter who was born in 1994, just after we sold the company. I was a bit older than most new dads. I had some money in the bank, a good home life, and I lived in a very supportive community.

Around the time my daughter turned four, I watched as she appeared to gravitate toward music and art. I saw her shyness—she wanted to perform in front of large audiences but she didn't think she was good enough. I decided to find a way to instill confidence and that "drive to be the best" in my daughter. I used to set aside every Saturday as "Daddy day" with her. Because she was only a little girl, she would easily got bored, and I had to find things that would hold her attention and keep her occupied. So I got creative and tried different things like roller skating, arcades, jungle gyms and even miniature golf.

One day, I hit the jackpot when I took her bowling. She immediately fell in love with it. She asked to go bowling again the very next day. Of course, I agreed. We started going every week and then at least two times a week. She eventually joined a league and had enough passion for bowling that she would go to the bowling alley just to practice.

After bowling for about 5 years, something interesting happened. Even though she was only nine years old, she was asked to participate in a state-wide tournament when an older kid dropped out of the competition at the last minute.

We drove for two hours that day to arrive at a beautiful bowling alley in a rural part of the state. When we arrived, the other girls were covering their mouths giggling and making remarks about her as she joined them. She may not have even been aware they were making fun of her. The tournament was about to start. My daughter was up first. She threw her first ball—it was a gutter ball. Her second ball was a gutter ball, too. I started to sweat and I thought that her self-confidence was shot, but her next ball was a strike. All of a sudden the other girls were ecstatic, and they cheered her on. That afternoon, she bowled three strikes and scored the highest she ever did.

And in the end, miraculously, her team won the state title. This was the first tournament title for the local bowling alley in thirty years. For my daughter, it was the beginning of making an important connection in life. She worked really hard, and as a result she truly experienced being the absolute best at something.

She learned so many lessons from that experience. Most importantly, winning had been instilled in her at a young age to the point that it became an expectation. She found something she loved, was willing to put in the hard work to be the best she could be, and she ultimately experienced the immeasurable reward of success. Today she maintains a

3.8 GPA at university and she's authored two books, one of which has been published. (Yes, Dad is bragging a little.)

****

This story can be applied to your company. When your company is focused on a positive outcome, the energy behind that positive outcome is much stronger. When the goal is to be #1, it becomes an ocean wave that breaks at the shore every single time. The momentum of the culture carries the company to success. The team is used to being #1. That is the winner's mentality!

Your Invisible Organization *will* prosper if you master the necessary skills, continue to learn, and are smart enough to get help when needed.

My company specializes in helping CEOs running companies of any size, get their mindset right before making the required changes to create the most profound effect on profits and operations. If you want more information on success coaching for CEOs, visit www.InvisibleOrganization.com/Resources .

4

The Outcomes You Will Enjoy
When Going Invisible

By transitioning to an Invisible Organization you will increase profits, reduce overhead and have a happy, fulfilled work force. By the end of this book you will have all the pieces in place for a successful Invisible Organization.

You may think I use the term *invisible* and *virtual* interchangeably, but they do have a different meaning. Being *invisible* refers to a company that provides their clients a customer experience that is frictionless and efficient while effortlessly delivering a superior product by an incredible staff. The word *virtual* just means that your staff is working from a remote location. A company that takes their broken processes and deploys them virtually is not an Invisible Organization.

An Invisible Organization has integrated highly efficient systems and standardized training. An Invisible Organization has reduced or eliminated their physical infrastructure and has very happy staff members who love their company and enjoy their jobs. Being virtual is just one component of being invisible.

Outcome #1: A New Way of Thinking

"The Invisible Organization Approach" means you are rethinking and restructuring your workflow, your training systems, your hiring systems and your sales/customer service staff functions so that they become part of a bigger, more holistic picture. By the time you're done reading this book, you'll *constantly* be looking for ways to scale your operations without the limitations you've had in the past. I know it can be done. I've managed the process, and I've see this work over and over again with small offices and large corporations. Wouldn't your company benefit if you were able to sell to prospects no matter where they lived? Wouldn't you prefer hiring the best staff in the world instead of having to stay within a thirty-mile radius of your office?

What if you could hire the best person possible no matter where they lived, without requiring them to move? This means they stay in their own community, their own home, and you don't pay moving expenses. How many times did you miss out on a qualified candidate because the move would have been too stressful for their family? With housing prices still not returned to their pre-crash levels, people can join your team without having to face a huge loss on their home. You can attract top salespeople without paying big base salaries or allocating office space for them. How is that possible? That's in chapter ten.

Outcome #2: A Streamlined and More Efficient Organization

Putting systems in place is a major part of developing your strategy to become more and more invisible. In order to put the right systems in place, you need to answer these questions:

- What will it take to extend your current operations outside your building?

- Are you already using web-based technology that runs in the cloud?

- Is your technology absolutely brand new?

- Are your business processes well defined to the point where they can be defined as a step-by-step sequence to get the desired result?

Go online now to www.InvisibleOrganization.com/Resources and take the full assessment to see just how close you are to being ready to transform your company.

The simplicity of a "system"

Creating a system is nothing more than writing down step-by-step an existing process that is working well. These days you don't even have to write it down. You can go to Jing. com and record your screen and your voice while running through all the processes you do. To make it even easier, you can then email the link of your recording to your virtual assistant in a foreign country and for a few dollars have the whole thing transcribed for you.

If you document what your staff does and perfect the step-by-step process, someone new can come along and be integrated into your training process almost instantly. They will simply need to follow those steps to learn how to do that particular job.

This is the core of the Invisible Organization: well-trained staff all having the same information, all trained to do things the same way, and all providing the same level of service to your clients.

Here are the key points:

1. Systemize what you know. Do you have an outline of what you do with every client?

2. Write out the steps you use. Debug it. Work out the kinks. Add to it. Enhance it. Perfect it. Lay down in detail everything you do.

3. Test it carefully with someone who doesn't know it and make sure your directions are clear.

4. Take your system and record the steps required to operate it, with software that teaches others.

What does a "system" look like when you are done?

It can be as simple as a list of procedures to accomplish a task. Let's say you want your bookkeeper to have a system that helps her make deposits when checks come in. Your system might simply be something like this:

1. Stamp check with company deposit stamp.

2. Record the amount of the check in QuickBooks under "Income" and note who it is from.

3. Go to the Invoice for that item and mark it paid. If there's more than one invoice, mark them all paid.

4. Put the check in the "checks" envelope and deposit at the bank on Wednesdays and Fridays.

Simply put, if your bookkeeper quit, you could have your new bookkeeper log into your virtual training environment and be up and running quickly because you built that training system. That's all it really is.

Of course, it can get far more complex than that. Ask all key staff members to write up their jobs. I required an operating guide (or a series of training videos created by my staff) for each and every position in the company that had processes and procedures, which made bringing on new staff far easier. By doing this you'll never have to train someone ever again.

Each person is responsible for updating his or her own training course.

When everyone is managing their own training environment, when all your systems are completely up-to-date, when everything is electronically stored off site and accessible instantly from anywhere, you have a perpetual self-training environment that is always ready to use.

Obviously, there is no "system" for creativity, and that was never implied. This is about making sure that every single operation of the company is carefully documented. That way, no one can threaten to quit while having too much leverage to force unreasonable requests.

Company culture and inspiring videos of you presenting the vision of your company can become part of your training system so that future hires can emerge with knowledge of your vision, your products, and your clients even before they start working.

Later in chapter six, I'll cover how to develop an easy-to-understand course that can be deployed virtually, to anyone, anywhere in the world using your documented job write-ups.

You've probably worked hard to optimize your sales process, to perfect the display of your merchandise or how your shop floor is run, and to debug the processes involved. By building a working system and training, you'll increase profits: your staff will work faster and more efficiently.

You'll see results almost immediately. The worries of bringing in new business are taken off your plate. You'll get more work done, attract more business, and you and your staff will enjoy life more.

When you have a clear vision of your company's goal and the type of clients you want to have, it will become easier to achieve. If you're reading this book, it means you are a visionary and have an open mind to explore new profitable opportunities. By going beyond any possible limitations of how you see your current business, you can take a fresh look at your resources and assets including how to hire the most amazing staff you can imagine. Most people would love to work from the comfort of their home, and when you are a fantastic employer, they will go to great lengths to support the success of the company.

Outcome #3: Happier, More Productive Staff

When Tony Robbins decided that it was time to apply these principles to his company, he saved a small fortune. Staff satisfaction and productivity increased, and Tony's company was able to reduce their leased space and associated overhead.

There is another benefit to having invisible staff. Staff members working at a physical facility are more likely to get sick when flu season starts. Think about it. The average person comes in contact with two or three people on his way to work: he picks up a latte at the coffee shop, drops his clothes off at the dry cleaners, and fills up his tank at the gas station.

Suppose there are a hundred people in the office who each met two or three people before they arrived at work. Chances are that at least a few of your staff members would get infected, and they would then unknowingly contaminate their coworkers.

By working at home, each person comes in contact with less people, and the risk of getting sick is reduced significantly. Comparing the sick days from the Invisible Organization I ran with the traditional company, I can tell from experience that staff members call in sick less when they work from home. They can use those days to go on vacation instead, which benefits the staff as well as the company. Your insurance company may give you discounts because there are less medical incidents, and if you are self-insured, you may notice a drop in doctor bills and prescription drugs.

And don't forget the soul-sucking commute that many people have to slug their way through twice a day. Could there be fewer car accidents and less stress too?

With the fresh perspective of this book, look at every aspect of your business and ask yourself, "In what areas can I apply *The Invisible Organization Approach?*

A simple assessment can be done by looking at each staff member and asking:

- Could he be productive working from home?

- Is his physical presence at the office really important? If yes, why?

- Would he experience saving his daily commute to and from the office as a benefit?

- Does he meet with clients face-to-face? Does he have to?

- Does he physically construct something that has to be passed on to the next person who adds to that physical product assembly?

- If our staff worked remotely, how much would we save on rent, electricity, supplies, etc.?

- Could the company function at a higher level by spending less time maintaining a facility, equipment or physical systems and more time on the actual final valuable product the company produces?

Carefully analyze each person's daily activities, their productivity, their personality, and the systems you currently have in place. Then evaluate what would be needed for each person to function remotely. Don't be quick to say, "Yes, he could work from home but...." Instead search for ways to *make* it possible, and you'll be greatly rewarded.

Take the full assessment at www.InvisibleOrganization.com/Resources. You will get results instantly.

After doing the full assessment, you might at first come to the conclusion that it's not possible to allow your complete staff to work from home or to change your business model. It may seem that there are no areas in your business that can be changed. If it's hard to identify any areas, it's probably because you're too close to your company.

Often people are so used to doing things a certain way that it's difficult to expand outside their comfort zone. That's why you need a third party viewpoint to show you what areas to inspect inside your company that have the potential to exist outside the office. This book will start the process. Attend a mastermind with CEO's running a virtual organization, and you'll see many others who have successfully transitioned their own companies and are happy to share their stories. You'll be amazed to discover how much more *is* possible if you take a step back and take a fresh approach.

The point is that having a work-from-home company will make staff happier and more productive. If that's not possible, then the tools used to enable work-from-home activities can also be deployed at your office. You will not get the massive savings on infrastructure that you would if they were working from home, but you will boost productivity with the best cloud-based solutions for the job.

Going invisible is a state of mind beyond sending people home. Even though it's true that it may not be feasible for every company to be fully virtual, they can function and be as efficient as an Invisible Organization, meaning they will be better companies with strong cultures, super-happy employees, and frictionless, productive environments.

SECTION THREE:

The CEO's Blueprint for Unlimited Expansion

5

Mapping Out the Plan

The only way you can build an Invisible Organization is by having the right virtual systems and cloud-based software in place. This will allow you to manage, monitor, track and improve the performance of the company. Everything must be interconnected, because that is what will make your Invisible Organization function at peak efficiency. It's one thing to operate virtually, but without connecting those virtual systems into a seamless flow of information from start to finish, you are creating friction and frustration for your staff.

To illustrate, imagine that your ears couldn't communicate with your brain. Whenever somebody told you something, the information would have to be written down by someone else so that you could read it and your brain could process the information. That is exactly what happens in your company when your CRM system doesn't communicate with you virtual call center, sales force or website. You're wasting time and money while frustrating your clients and staff.

Good systems are critically important, allowing your team to be more productive and your organization more efficient. Great people count, and you want to take good care of those who support the organization. The goal is to appear to your clients as a large and powerful, caring and supportive company even though you don't own huge buildings. Remember that a well-run, tightly organized company delivers on its promises, provides a reliable customer experience, and appears much larger than it is.

Some systems are so common that you may not even realize they're systems. Take email, for example. It's a simple way to communicate; yet at the same time, when properly organized with a folder structure, it can work fine to store research and client information for very small projects. On the other hand, without a proper system in place, lost emails can cause a loss of productivity and upset your clients. There are many specialized cloud-based systems that have become quite popular and have proven to be very valuable. The decisions you make now are critical, as they will determine the future scalability of your company.

Before you start researching the systems you will need, it is best to start with creating an information flow diagram. The diagram will give you much insight. In many organizations information is duplicated needlessly or extra work has to be done because the systems aren't connected, which of course reduces productivity.

The Nuts and Bolts

Let's start with an example. In this example, leads come in from different sources, and from that point there are several possible ways to sell a low cost product and sell the client higher priced add-ons. This is how that might look:

In this example which shows the lead flow of one of the companies I ran, every lead created a contact record in the CRM system. A person would call and buy a $299 seat for the three-hour webinar that taught how to create a business in a box. During the webinar, the client would get the education he paid for plus be exposed to our high-end business training system, which was available for $3,997. Once the sale of the higher-end product was made, the sales data moved to the accounting software for credit card processing and to the commission engine for sorting and disbursing the commission splits. Then a time sequence was triggered after the sale where customer service checked to make sure the client was happy and getting what he had paid for.

If the prospect didn't buy, then based on the source of the lead (email lead, telephone lead or affiliate lead), he was sent a survey and a down-sell offer or his contact information was forwarded to the sales force. In many cases the lead was being sent to all three in sequence. The CRM system was designed to manage this sorting and sequencing of the offers automatically.

At each step of the way, the prospect's record was maintained and updated with everything that he did before and after he turned into a client. Each communication, payment and inquiry was tracked, sorted and stored.

In this simple example, the company used three different cloud-based systems: a CRM system, the webinar presentation system, and the virtual call center. The three were interconnected to insure frictionless interactions between the (potential) client and the company staff. (We'll go into each one of these in great detail, so just keep reading.)

Now it's your turn.

If we were working on this together, I would ask you:

- Where do your leads come from?

- How do they flow through your company?

- Do your leads go to an email auto-responder or to your salespeople?

Now that you have the list of all your lead sources and where those leads go, let's create a flow diagram. By far the most important element for the success of your Invisible Organization is to integrate the dataflow as seamlessly as possible. This requires a full understanding of how leads flow through your company, how they convert to sales, and what happens at each step of the process. (This same information will be needed to train new staff.)

Let's take one lead flow type (magazine ads, radios commercials, TV commercials, Internet, etc.) at a time and map its path through your company. You'll likely have a dozen different lead types, each one with a list of sources. The next step is to see what actions must be taken based on the lead flow type. An Internet lead should be handled differently than a phone lead from a radio commercial. Write down the sequence of follow-up actions for each type of lead so that you have a collection of these paths.

After you've done this, notice how those lead streams combine into a single database. Ideally certain data items trigger a timed sequence of offers (auto-responder) to your prospects. By carefully designing a flow diagram of all leads, clients, contracts or other work products through your business, you will exactly see what type of systems are needed.

After evaluating the different options, you'll have to decide which system meets your needs, fits your budget, and will integrate well with the rest of your lead flow chain. There will always be better and more sophisticated systems available, but it's the interconnectedness of the entire environment that will determine how well your Invisible Organization will function. Besides lead and sales flow, you will want to create a strategy for using, scaling and expanding your company.

It's not easy, but it is simple to understand once you've plotted out lead flow a few times on your own!

If you have trouble figuring out how this works, go to www.InvisibleOrganization.com/Resources and get some assistance. This is a crucial step since it drives the entire build-out of your cloud-based system.

- Is the system you use now a true CRM system, or is it a combination of several different databases scattered around the company?

- Can your current CRM system handle the different lead flow types?

- Does it take the follow-up actions needed to optimize your sales?

You will gain great efficiency when all data is stored and accessible in a central system that communicates with all other systems. Let's see what the ideal CRM system looks like!

The Heart of Your Invisible Organization — Your CRM System

Every company needs a professional Customer Relationship Management system, CRM for short. As your company grows, your CRM becomes your master client database with tentacles that flow throughout the company. It can connect with other systems by integrating the client data you collect, and it can be used at every level inside the company—from the sales floor to the CEO's office.

Your CRM system is your central hub that tracks all customer and prospect interactions. The right CRM system can be connected with your web pages so that each click of the mouse on the Internet can be tracked and categorized with a set of specific actions that take place with each client interaction. When coupled with accounting software, the tracking of a prospect who then becomes a client can be made seamless. Since customer service records every interaction with the client and makes notes of each product they purchase or inquire about, your CRM system is a record of the entire prospect-client life cycle.

CRM systems are highly programmable. They can run your marketing programs and respond to prospect and client inquiries. By having a well-thought-out CRM strategy, you can "listen" to all your social media identities and catalog those actions. You can act on any of them directly, you can provide valuable information to your prospects and clients as requested, and you can build management dashboards to see real-time what is going on with your promotions, response rates, and revenue. Some CRM systems have thousands of add-ons, which make them extremely useful but also very complex. It's best to start with your current needs and then add features as they are required.

Because your CRM system is cloud-based, your staff can access it from anywhere in the world. By connecting it with virtual call center software, your call center staff can work from the comfort of their own homes, take calls from customers, and enter real-time conversation details in the CRM system. Some CRM systems require a third party application for order entry and look-up, but in most cases this feature is included. Some CRM systems like Infusionsoft, for example, link to accounting software, while other CRM systems contain complete order processing systems. If you are already using accounting software that processes your orders for you, it may only be necessary to link it with your CRM system. That way you'll avoid entering data twice.

Since it requires skill to set up the connections correctly, having a CRM architect or consultant design your virtual environment is extremely useful. The money you'll invest in a CRM architect will come back to you with dividends for many years to come. Well-designed and implemented systems will be adapted more readily by your staff than a convoluted and difficult-to-use system. This will smooth the always rocky transition.

Sales people and beginning micro-preneurs are generally the heaviest users of CRM software. They are not software people; they only want to learn what they need to do their job. When you implement or change the CRM system, you'll likely get resistance. Your sales people may start kicking and screaming and refuse to use the new software.

I've implemented CRM software for five different companies, and I observed every time that the implementation was painful and took longer than expected. Despite the fact that I ran a CRM software publishing company and knew more about the problems implementing these types of systems in many different environments, it wasn't easy. But I knew for certain that if management would be persistent with training and encouragement, staff would soon find it invaluable—and they did!

The consolidation of data in one environment and the integration of all systems in your company revolve around your CRM system. CRM vendors know this and go to great lengths to make sure they build products that easily import and export data while having APIs for just about any purpose.

Check carefully and pay attention to fees. APIs (Application Programming Interface) can enable software developers to add functionality to a system. Some APIs and extensions can cost a small fortune. InfusionSoft and SalesForce.com both have large libraries of add-on programs for very specialized purposes all built with APIs. Both InfusionSoft and SalesForce are powerful and popular CRM products, even though they are relatively expensive compared to other CRM systems. Your technical staff will need to evaluate which one would best meet your company's needs. If you want assistance in assessing what system would be best suited for your company, contact us directly at www.InvisibleOrganization.com/Resources.

The most powerful integrated CRM system for consulting, coaching and training companies that I've run across is www.Kazeli.com. If you sell information and work with clients, Kazeli is an excellent solution. Besides having a rich feature set, it works with many different products and can be customized endlessly. There are interfaces already built in for several virtual call center software products, so you can share information without additional customization and more can be added if needed. Besides the traditional CRM functionality, it has a complete file sharing system similar to Google Drive, which eliminates the need for a separate system. InfusionSoft and Kazeli both monitor and track all prospect and client activities on your website. If your CRM doesn't connect with your website, than that data must be entered manually. Kazeli also has a survey module that extends to your website. The survey results are automatically stored with the contact record of the client. This is valuable, because it adds texture to your relationship with your clients. The more you know about them, the better you can target and serve them.

Complex and powerful marketing programs can easily be orchestrated through Kazeli's campaign manager. I have experience accomplishing all this and more with Kazeli. There may be other systems that can provide these services, but this is the only one I know well and can recommend from personal experience.

If your company is built on a hodge-podge of independent systems that have to be strung together with bailing wire and bubble gum, you will never be able to grow. When your systems are disjointed, training becomes more complex, efficiency drops, and the information flow becomes more complicated. That is why interconnectedness is more important than functionality.

Some companies have inside and outside sales reps, while others don't have telephone sales reps at all. Years ago when I worked in the electronics distribution business, I realized that business clients prefer to place their orders with salespeople who can take them to lunch. If that is how your company works, your CRM software should extend to the cellphone of your sales rep, allowing him to take notes while with the client.

Your Virtual Call Center Software

A virtual call center can manage all incoming calls, route and record them. The incoming phone number can provide demographic, geographic and profiling data of the caller. This gives your salesperson the ability to know in advance if he'll be talking to an important prospect or a student doing research. These systems are simple for staff members to use. When the phone rings, they accept the call with a click of their mouse, while a box with all the data of the caller pops up on their computer screen and flows automatically into the CRM software. This provides invaluable management reporting on the origin and result of each call.

If you don't have telephone sales reps and won't need a call center in the future either, you can skip this section. But even if you have a few reps working on the phone, this piece of technology coupled with your CRM system will be invaluable.

There are two key components to a virtual call center. It's good to understand what both are and what they do.

1. **The call monitoring software.** If you are using toll-free numbers, the company you lease your lines from provides the monitoring system. Your phone numbers are delivered through a software interface so that you can monitor all call activity.

Here's an example of an incoming call management screen showing exactly when calls are coming in. Remember, these calls are being routed to homes around the world where reps answer those calls and close them or deliver a service.

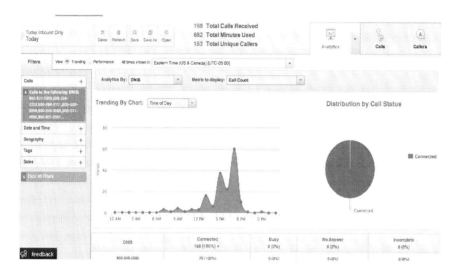

This screen illustrates your calling trend. It shows you the peaks, which allows you to schedule your work force accordingly. As you can see, this day the peak calling time was about 6:00 p.m., and nearly sixty calls came in simultaneously.

2. The call routing software directs the incoming calls to your reps in the order you decide. There are two different types of call routing systems: one requires a landline while the other requires a fast Internet connection because the calls come in via computer.

First, determine if your staff will be using landlines to accept incoming calls or their computers with a headset connected to the USB port. Virtual call center systems that are designed to operate with standard phone lines may require you to lease a certain number of trunk lines (dedicated phone lines connected to your individual account). The downside of a system like this is that if a call load spikes past the number of trunk lines, callers can't get connected. Trunk lines are expensive and must be in place before you start a campaign. My experience comes from high volume phone calls from radio ads, but any incoming phone calls can be handled with the same system.

PC phone-based virtual call centers are more versatile; cost less to use, and require no set number of leased phone lines in advance. (While Macs can be used, PCs seem to work best with these systems.) The downside of this system is that you're dependent on the speed, strength and reliability of the Internet connection. Management may decide to pay for fast Internet service for their staff. Yet if there are Internet problems that can't be overcome, there are only two options:

- Change sales reps.

- Change virtual call center systems.

Virtual call center systems have extensive features and vary in price points. You can get an up-to-date list of the best virtual call center systems to start your own due diligence at www.InvisibleOrganization.com/Resources.

As you explore the different options, make sure the software you select can accommodate your current and future needs. Create a resource allocation table that has a list of your current staff by department, and approximate your growth for the next three years. It will look like this:

Division/Resource	Current Staff	12 months	24 months	36 months
Inbound Sales	8	14	20	30
Customer Service	4	8	12	16
Tech Support	2	3	5	8
Marketing	1	1	2	2
Outbound Sales	2	3	4	5
# Incoming phone lines	16	28	40	60

The above data helps to estimate the size of your future system needs. The real estate expenses to grow a company like the example in the allocation table above would escalate quickly. Just think how much you'll save in rent alone when you're growing an Invisible Organization. You may be paying for "seats" on a monthly basis as part of your system cost, depending on which system you choose.

Consult with your CRM vendor to help you configure your CRM system with your virtual call center to make sure it fits the needs of your organization. As you grow, a CRM administrator, who will make sure that the database continues to run smoothly, will become a valuable addition to your team.

Once you have your call center set up, you can closely monitor all your incoming calls and listen to the call recordings. You can also barge in and listen silently.

In the screen below, you can see how easy it is to determine where your calls are coming from, which reps are taking calls, and which radio stations are pulling the most calls if you are doing radio advertising.

The DNIS is the toll-free line your calls are coming in from, with the name of the commercial right below the number. This is useful if you are running various commercials simultaneously, because you can track which one is most successful.

You can see where the calls come from, who answered them, and the duration of each call. If a conversation took place, you can listen to it from the dashboard. In this example, the company doesn't have enough staff and the overflow calls go to voicemail.

Closing the Loop:
Getting Staff Productive and Tracking Their Activity

If most of your staff is taking inbound sales calls or dealing with customer service, you pretty much know what they are doing and when they are scheduled to work. Yet overall it would be good to see how your staff is spending their time.

One tool I've found to be very valuable is a time tracker. It allows you to see the whole team's activities on one screen, and it can take screen-shots during the day. The myth that you can't hold your staff accountable when they work from home dissipates with tools like this. It is a voluntary system, meaning your staff has to turn it on to track their time, yet you can make it a requirement if they want to get paid.

There are time tracking tools available at www.InvisibleOrganization.com/Resources

How to Deliver Your Products

Next it's important to recognize the different sales channels you use and how each one delivers its products. If changes in the delivery of your products need to be made with the addition of virtual systems, build that into your plan.

If your goal is to be invisible but you have a physical manufacturing facility, you may consider using third party fulfillment. There are three reasons why you should use a fulfillment center that produces and ships your products:

1. To save money
2. To improve processing time
3. To increase staff efficiency

With an outside fulfillment vendor, you don't need to employ staff to fulfill. The vendor will ship the product for you. Using cloud-based systems, all your packing slips and shipping labels can be printed remotely. There are many fulfillment companies varying from small local companies to vast international product manufacturers to whom you can outsource your entire physical operation. We used a fulfillment center to duplicate the floppy disk with our software. We had the manuals printed in bulk. They labeled the disks, put them in sleeves, packed them in boxes with the manuals, and shipped them to our clients.

If you sell an information product, all you have to do is make sure your CRM systems can deliver the content to clients after they pay. Obviously, you can design a series of marketing messages to upsell additional products and services.

Take a closer look at your company and see where there are opportunities to innovate with virtual technology. In many cases, virtual software vendors will show you exactly how to apply their products to your company. They want you to fully understand the capabilities of their platforms.

The information in this chapter provides you with the basics. The best solution for *your* company depends on your operation. It requires someone with experience in virtual systems and business models to help you do a full analysis of the systems you'll need to optimize your efficiency, productivity and profitability.[1]

IMPORTANT NOTE: The specific products and systems I mention in this chapter are by no means a complete list of

---

1 If you need help, contact the author at Mitch@InvisibleOrganization.com.

all the available options. Some of the resources may even be out of date shortly after this book is published. Please check www.InvisibleOrganization.com/Resources for the latest recommendations.

6

How I Trained an Entire Company Using Automated Systems

Training your staff properly is critical to the success of any company, but in an Invisible Organization it is even more important to train them with perfection from the beginning. Standardized training insures that everyone "sings from the same song sheet," using the established vocabulary of the company every time and delivering the tested, proven benefits of your products and services. Improper or non-standardized training leads to "creativity," meaning that each person may tell clients something different. Of course, this isn't what you want because this leads to inconsistency in every area of your business. The best process would be to use automated training tools to bring new staff up to speed quickly.

Setting Up a Training System

Ideally, every new salesperson should be trained by the very best, most experienced sales executive. Unfortunately, that person may not be available forever or broadly to everyone, so their lessons need to be captured and delivered in an automated way. Your best salespeople's most successful calls must be recorded to build a library of available training calls. While that is a good start, it won't be very effective unless you design and implement learning assessments with it. When a new hire has listened to a call or has watched a video, he has to pass a test to go on to the next lesson. If not, he has to go back and start over.

A good training system can be highly customized to house different types of media for many different sources and allow for comprehensive exam setup with online scoring and feedback. It also lets management know where each trainee is in the curriculum, how each person is scoring, if he is ahead or behind schedule, and when he's expected to have completed the training.

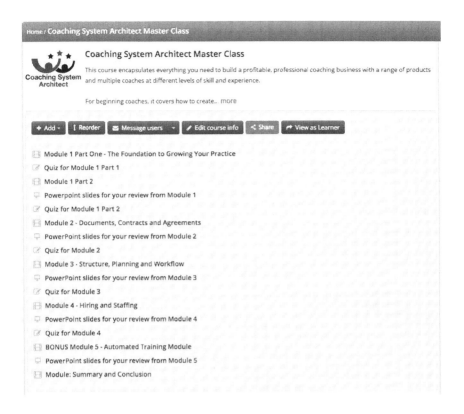

This is an example of a training center. Each course has built-in assessments for every stage of the learning cycle. The courseware should be created by the most skilled people, or at least guided by them, to ensure that you're developing the highest level of training.

The Training Environment that Guarantees Success

A great lesson may last thirty to forty-five minutes and be broken into seven to ten chunks of knowledge or concepts. Each concept is explained using a video or write-up. Examples are great for illustrating new concepts as well. Then each chunk of knowledge is followed by a test. Sometimes the test may be short (two or three questions), and other times it may require eight to twelve multiple choice or essay questions to answer.

A good training environment has rules which dictate how and when a person moves to the next step. If you pass the test, you get access to the next lesson. You can program your environment so it won't allow passage from one question to the next if the answer is incorrect. You can require a person to re-watch the video or reread the material until they score 100%.

At the end of the process, when the new hire has passed through the entire program and has completed the module, you can print a certificate that can be posted on the wall or you can give them a visual token that can be displayed on their LinkedIn page or their email signature to provide the social proof that they are competent or even an expert in a particular area.

The system will show you exactly who is making progress.

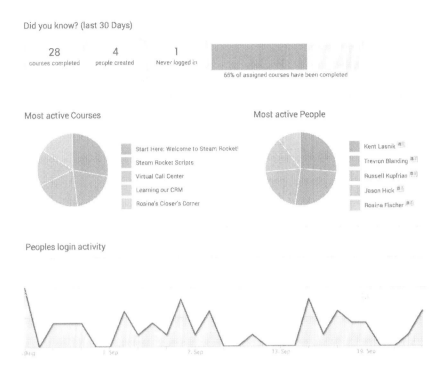

Did you know? (last 30 Days)

28	4	1
courses completed	people created	Never logged in

65% of assigned courses have been completed

Most active Courses

- Start Here: Welcome to Steam Rocket!
- Steam Rocket Scripts
- Virtual Call Center
- Learning our CRM
- Rosina's Closer's Corner

Most active People

- Kent Lasnik
- Trevion Blanding
- Russell Kupfrian
- Jason Hick
- Rosina Fischer

Peoples login activity

The above screen shows the number of people that logged in every day and which courses they took. It also shows the number of courses completed.

You'll need training for every department. I'm using sales only as an example. This training system can be applied to any department, any topic, and any company.

When the new hire has completed his virtual training, the sales manager takes over and insures that each new staff member can deliver the sales script or presentation smoothly and efficiently. Generally the sales script has been crafted by sales management who has revised it to become even more powerful after it was tested and modified based on what did and didn't work. The less "creative" a salesperson is, the faster and more efficiently he will close a sale. When I use the term "creative" I simply mean that a person who follows the script exactly as he was trained statistically has a higher closing rate than those who don't. A central repository is required to house the latest selling and support documents, which requires a centralized document storage solution.

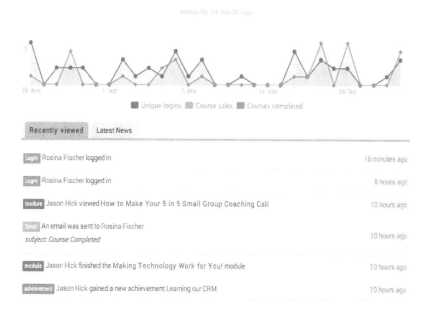

Then the training process is supplemented with tools like Join.me, where you can watch your potential new sales trainee operate your systems while you look over his shoulder. This is one of the last steps of the training.

Using the Power of an LMS

According to Wikipedia, a Learning Management System (LMS) is a software application for the administration, documentation, tracking, reporting and delivery of e-learning education courses or training programs.

There are several companies that offer Learning Management Systems, each with different features and price points. From my experience working with several of them, in the end it comes down to two things: the time it will take you to create the course, and then the price they charge for use of their system. For example, one LMS requires that the lessons be recorded in their studio and then assembled by their editing team.

If you are selling a low-cost e-course, a simple solution may work, but when it comes to training your staff, you need something with more teeth.

There are three types of training:

1. "Old school" DVD streaming video

The student sits passively and watches videos to learn. The student can wander off, check e-mail or take a phone call while the video runs. There are membership websites where you can store videos and show them in sequence. Even though it could be a solution for small companies, it lacks something very important: the ability to *interact*.

2. Interactive courseware

The big advantage of interactive courseware is that it increases comprehension. "Graduation" from an interactive course will insure that your new staff member really understands the training material. You could set up a cloud-based system with a full-blown course, sequencing videos, audios, PowerPoint presentations and just about anything you can show on your screen. After each segment a test must be passed in order to move to the next module.

This option doesn't require large sums of money or many months to produce. The results are excellent and can be built quickly, assuming you have a library of reference material available.

It's important to track the progress of your students. Many systems allow you to see who has completed each of the training modules, where they are in the process, the pace at which they are learning, and their scoring on the material. It's very easy to spot the enthusiastic and focused students in an environment like this.

Several systems send an alert when the student has not visited the course materials after a number of days. The supervisor will be informed if a staff member is not sticking to the training schedule. (This is also very useful when you use this system for coaching and a coach is guiding a client through the course material he has to study on his own before the next coaching session.)

Another major advantage of interactive courseware is that any course you create can be turned into a product. The best of breed allows you to build courses that can be repurposed as paid programs with a few adjustments. So as you build your training course, keep in the back of your mind that your are creating a product, too.

LMSs usually contain extensive course building tools, and many are easy to learn and use. It's smart to get some help building these systems since you want the training to be up quickly and be high quality. Get someone who is an expert at LMS implementation to help you organize your materials and populate your environment.

3. Virtual Reality Training

The most effective, comprehensive, and expensive type of training is virtual, where the new hire embarks upon a new course as if he's walked onto the Holodeck from *Star Trek* and builds a personal relationship with his instructor.

As the training starts, full video images appear live and interactive. These are pre-recorded videos designed to be used at different times in the training process. As your new hire is led through the material, his video instructor appears to be interacting live and in real time. It's not like watching a video. The system is so beautifully designed that if the virtual instructor asks the trainee to look at a chart, the trainee will see him standing there, shifting his legs or even checking his iPhone while waiting for the answer, but it's all a recording. At the same time, a team of people can be on standby to answer questions live in a chat box.

When the student answers the question asked by the system, it then switches to the next video based on the response of that student. The virtual "instructor" provides instant feedback and guides the new hire to a different part of the lesson based on his answers. Virtual reality training is expensive to build and implement, but it results in the highest level of learning and transference of skills. While not actually a live instructor, the interaction feels live to the trainee. This makes the course more enjoyable and keeps his attention fixed. No one walks away from an interactive virtual reality training course—there is too much interaction, and the course will not allow it.

There are dozens of LMS (Learning Management Systems) available, and each one has its own strengths and weaknesses. If you are heading down this path, visit www.InvisibleOrganization.com/Resources and we'll help select the best system for you.

7

Interconnectedness Smashes Friction and Boosts Profits

The most important aspect of a frictionless operation is that data isn't duplicated. The data must be available automatically everywhere it is needed and accessible to every relevant staff member. How do you find and select the best virtual tools?

I want to introduce you to a host of different corporate solutions that can greatly improve your operations. Most of the systems you've chosen in the past were likely selected because of their functionality and not for their connectivity, since you used them as isolated systems. I recommend high-functionality systems with the emphasis on connectivity, this will allow you to create a frictionless organization.

Working with Accounting Software

In any organization with salespeople, commissions are usually part of the picture. This is a fairly complex and interwoven system of who gets what for which clients and when. If calculating commissions has been delegated to your accounting staff, get them involved in this process. Consider having your CRM system do it for you.

Sales should flow through your CRM system, which has all your clients' information readily available including who booked the sale. Build a commission engine into your CRM that will do all the calculations for you, including returns. A well-designed system will even take into account how commissions are transferred between reps. For example, when reps are fired and their clients need to be reassigned or when reps change departments, they may receive legacy commission on past clients. A good commission tracking system should handle such type of cases with no problem.

Some companies have isolated their CRM system for leads only. Once a lead becomes a client, then that data is duplicated in an accounting system. While not ideal, it's complicated to switch, so for now let's leave that alone. After you've made your conversion to virtual, you can determine exactly what it takes to combine the two systems. Once again, this is more for your VP Finance or Controller to decide with you, but I want to stress that it should all be one world of data. Both prospect and client tracking should be combined so that your reps deliver a higher level of service *and* close more prospects.

Expense Accounting

All companies have executives that fill out expense reports. Those expense reports need to be accounted for, and reimbursements need to be made.

This is an example of a process that needs to be connected to your accounting software, not your lead or client systems. There are applications like www.Concur.com that are very well done. As this is an area where the expertise and knowledge of your financial systems are very relevant, it's best to involve your CFO in the decision-making process.

I highlight some of the best expense reporting tools on my website for you: www.InvisibleOrganization.com/Resources.

Storing Your Critical Corporate Documents

Every company needs to store and categorize its business documents and contracts, and a virtual organization is no exception. A basic system would be to have a cloud-based file storage system like www.Dropbox.com. Dropbox is a remote, private, and secure drive that allows you to store your documents in the cloud and gives you the possibility to give permission to certain staff members to share folders.

Another option would be to use document management software like Confluence. You can see a more detailed description here: http://www.atlassian.com/Confluence. It's the best mix of cost effectiveness and functionality that I have found as of this writing.

The document management you choose must have these features:

- It must be secure.

- It must have an audit trail for Security and Exchange Commission (SEC) compliance should you ever need it.

- It must have version control.

- It must be accessible from any device anywhere.

Without those features you are shortchanging your company and putting your valuable information in danger. Unauthorized access to sensitive documents could destroy a company from the inside out.

A good document manager makes everything accessible while preventing older versions from overwriting newer versions of the same documents. With Confluence, departmental portals can be created. That way marketing can have their finished work available to the company and sales can store their client presentations, scripts and customer proposals without concern that others will see their work. You can store meeting notes, collaborate with team members on documents, get notifications when documents change, manage tasks, assign work to team members, and even link several hundred add-ons. It's worth exploring this powerful and inexpensive solution to organizing and managing your documents.

Many CRM systems can act as a document and file manager storing your correspondence with clients. A good CRM system will allow you to store specific documents related to a client on the client record so all client-centric information is in one place.

Electronic Signatures — Faster Than FedEx

You no longer need physical signatures for contracts to be admissible as evidence in court—electronic signatures are fully acceptable. Electronic signatures save time, and since your signed documents are secure in the cloud, you can access them from anywhere and can't lose them. There are several companies who provide this service. I've used www.EchoSign.com. It is reliable and easy to use. There are several more options available on my website.

A copy of the signed documents should be stored in your CRM. The actual signed document should also remain in the cloud-based archive.

This is how it works:

1. You set up a departmental database of all contracts and agreements that clients and staff members need to sign. Arrange them securely so that every department only has access to their own specific documents.

2. After you upload and send the document with the request for an electronic signature, the system tracks its delivery.

3. The system is relentless if it doesn't receive the requested signature. It resends the request until the document is signed and will notify you of the status.

4. If a client says, "I never received the email," you can simply resend the link to the signature page.

5. Once the document is signed, the system automatically sends it to the next person to sign if multiple, sequential signatures are required.

6. If all parties have signed, the system sends out an email that the completed signed document is available for download.

7. The document is stored securely and can only be accessed by designated account holders. Every document can be given a security level, so salespeople can only see their own contracts while management can see all sales contracts.

Having a system for electronic signatures is ideal, because it's simple and fast. The client doesn't have to print out any documents to fax or mail. He can sign the contract with a click of his mouse. It can't get much easier.

Killer Customer Service and Tech Support

In the world we live in, it's all about keeping clients happy. Whether they have general questions, complaints or problems that need to be resolved, all these inquiries need to be handled. As you probably know from your own experience, there is nothing more frustrating than bad customer service. (In the next chapter, I'll explain how to provide six-star customer service.) Accelerated resolution of issues is the key to happy clients, and there's no better tool than an automated system.

There are several excellent cloud-based applications for customer service management. One of the more popular is www.Zendesk.com, a company-wide cloud-based help desk system. There are others you can choose from on www.InvisibleOrganization.com/Resources, but I will use ZenDesk.com as an example to highlight what a good help desk system should be able to do.

One of the most compelling features of Zendesk is that it builds a knowledge base from the questions clients ask. That knowledge base can create a public help forum with answers to questions that have been asked before. The questions are indexed, so they are easy to find and searchable with key words from your website. As your company expands, this knowledge base will continue to grow and can reduce the number of incoming calls.

Just imagine how much money you'll save if you can circumvent 10% of the incoming support calls with a knowledge-based information portal. Your savings will be worth the investment you made in the software. Over time this percentage will increase and cut down the number of support tickets even more.

This is also a great resource for your own tech support staff, as they will have access to all the answers provided in the past. There is also an internal tool that allows junior tech support people to ping a senior staff member with an instant message for quick resolution of a more advanced problem.

Zendesk also has a mobile service app that allows you to accept incoming inquiries from Facebook and other social media channels. Plus the chat feature can avoid long conversations with clients who are in the mood to talk. All these options are designed to save you money by preventing your clients or prospects from calling.

Clients appreciate it when the agent is familiar with their case before they have even started the conversation. That's why it's critically important to have all of your systems integrated. Since Zendesk can be linked to different CRM systems, all data about clients can be found in one place and be accessed from anywhere in the world, as long as there is an Internet connection. With tools like Zendesk there really is no need to build your own systems.

Project Management In the Cloud

Project management is a complex and comprehensive topic. Having the right project management software that integrates with the rest of your environment will make sharing information far easier. Cloud-based project management software has evolved to the point where it matches the sophistication of more traditional high-end products like Microsoft Project. While there will always be specialized tools for vertical markets, cloud-based systems are evolving quickly and should be part of your path to virtualizing your organization. With programmers and engineers working remotely, cloud-based project management software is critical to keeping work groups up-to-date.

This is not a tool that fits into the CRM hub system since it's generally an "engineering-only" tool. The important point, and the reason it's in this book as a mention, is because server-based project management is no longer the best way to go. Once you are in the cloud, all engineering, documentation and testing staff have easy access.

Schedule Management

One of the most time saving tools I have ever deployed as a busy executive is an online schedule manager. Of course, this will never replace a competent assistant, but it's a great tool! It's a cloud-based system that allows someone who wants to schedule an appointment on your calendar. You set up in advance the duration of each time slot and your availability. Because it's connected to your personal calendar, time slots will only show when they are available. After somebody has booked an appointment, he fills out a short interview form so that you know what the call will be about. It's simple, powerful, and very inexpensive. The tool I use is called www.TimeTrade.com, and it's designed to be used from a web page, an email, or even a Twitter or Facebook post. To the outside world it's a simple link, but to you, it's your virtual assistant.

Here's where it gets interesting. If you have a team of recruiters or service professionals like message therapists, chiropractors or tutors, you can set up a corporate account. By allowing clients to book their own appointments online, you can reduce the workload of the receptionist. There is even a feature that will remind clients of their appointment. It also works great if clients want to schedule or reschedule an appointment, as we discussed in the previous chapter. As a management tool, you can see everyone's appointments from a dashboard so you know what's going on in your organization, and the activity level of each staff member can be monitored. There are other appointment scheduling tools like www.TimeTrade.com. Some are specialized for specific vertical markets, but this is the best one for low-cost, highly customized group and individual scheduling.

You can go to www.InvisibleOrganization.com/Resources to see other scheduling tools that I recommend.

Planning Shifts

When you get up to about ten people in a department and you are supporting clients for more than a single eight-hour shift, shift-scheduling can get very complex. Depending on your type of business, you cannot effectively manage shifts without a system, especially as your team grows. If you own a retail store and want to keep track of your employees' calendar so that you know who is in the store/s and at what time/s, this is for you.

It can minimize overtime by more efficiently scheduling staff in shifts. It's also a valuable tool to use if you have multiple technical support organizations around the world in different time zones. My favorite product is www.ShiftPlanning.com. It is simple to use but very powerful, giving you a lot of control over your workforce. It links to your payroll systems, and it functions as a check-in/check-out time clock. Businesses that use shift-planning software include:

- Restaurants

- Retail Stores

- Health Care

- Police/Fire Services

Because staff members can log in whenever they want to check schedules, it makes everyone's life easier. They can pick open shifts, make shift changes and even trade shifts with other staff members. In general, scheduling vacation time is a nightmare, particularly around the holidays. The staff can request vacation time in the system for management to approve. With shift planning software, management defines the overtime rules, vacation rules, and staff changes that can be enabled. It interfaces with your H/R software and payroll. As it serves as your time clock, it's easy to see who is working. For remote owners of businesses with multiple locations, overall control is essential yet very easy with this type of software.

As you can see, there is a rich selection of cloud-based tools to help you manage your organization. While the focus has been on virtual organizations, all of these tools can be deployed inside a physical facility as well. There's almost no reason to use more traditional "server-based" systems, which require a large up-front capital investment and on-going support, maintenance, upgrades and service. Instead, a per-seat monthly fee that is variable and based entirely on the size of your organization is the utmost in flexibility. There's no simpler solution that will control overhead and scale to unlimited levels.

This is a visual example of an Invisible Organization that fully utilizes cloud-based systems. There are many valuable resources to facilitate your needs:

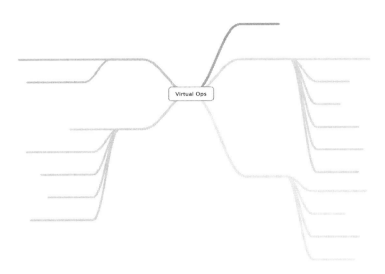

Every department has its specific requirements to accomplish its goals. Before you do your research, carefully document the specific functionality of the software you currently use so you'll know the tasks your new environment must be able to handle.

Start to move away from your conventional systems slowly while transitioning into your virtual environment, but run them in parallel for a few weeks to make sure you are getting the same results. Odds are that you will want to abandon your conventional systems and move to your new cloud-based environment more quickly. Make the break when you know your new cloud-based environment can handle your needs. Now you are becoming invisible!

For example, if you have a stand-alone CRM system that doesn't interact with the other applications you are current-ly using, you will need to migrate the data into a new CRM environment. Run both side by side to insure there are no errors. This way you'll prevent putting the company at risk with a new system that doesn't yet work. When you make the break and are completely shifted to a virtual environment, your data will be more available throughout the organization. You are headed in the right direction.

Start sending staff home to see if work and productivity are up to par. Your team may be reluctant in the beginning since they may not be comfortable with the new systems right away. No one likes change, but by providing good training, making the transition gradual, and helping staff to understand the value, you can reduce their resistance to a minimum. Once you become invisible, your expansion can no longer be contained by walls. The sky is the limit!

Ideally you would start from scratch with a full systems design. It will save you a fortune on conversion. Most people reading this book already have their infrastructure in place. In that case the best approach will be to run parallel systems, which will allow you to test your cloud-based environment before you fully make the switch, ensuring that your new systems give you the same or better results. Your focus needs to be on improving what you have and getting to the next step as carefully as possible.

Plan for double the time you initially thought it would take to accomplish a fully tested and replicated system, even if you hire a consultant. Don't be surprised when problems surface—they always do, so just keep moving forward. The overall advantage will be worth it. Keep the end game in mind: increased efficiency, reduced expenses, insanely happy staff members and a better customer experience than ever before. In the process of changing your operating basis to a virtual one, watch carefully to see if there are areas that need improvement.

Years ago I worked with a company to upgrade their infrastructure. As we started to dissect their legacy systems, we discovered something interesting. There were actual calculation mistakes that had been in their systems for years. Imagine the shock of the business owner and the staff who ran his internal systems when they discovered errors in the way sales and traffic statistics were calculated! That's why a full data-mapping plan is so useful. It shows you the source of data that some people take for granted. What happens if simple mistakes have negatively affected the way you've viewed your web traffic or sales statistics for years? Take the time to recheck everything while you are transitioning to your cloud-based systems.

Use this information as the start of a powerful internal movement to improve productivity, reduce costs, and thrill your staff as more of them can now work as much as they want from anywhere in the world. These are the basic tools of the Invisible Organization, and when integrated properly and completely, clients see a unified, happy workforce that gets things done quickly and efficiently.

Before you choose a product in any of the above categories, go to www.InvisibleOrganization.com/Resources to see a rich selection of products with my ratings. Additionally, if you would like help evaluating any of these products, feel free to contact me.

SECTION FOUR:

Marketing Strategies Optimized for Your Invisible Organization

8

Optimizing Your Marketing to Fully Exploit Your Invisible Organization

Marketing for the most part is marketing, no matter what type of company you have. When you operate in an Invisible Organization, you can take advantage of being able to scale quickly because you don't need real estate.

For example, let's say you want to run a very large marketing campaign that requires 100 new telesales people. Could you quickly hire 100 top sales superstars, provision all the equipment including computers, phones, cubicles, chairs and build out the facility? It's not likely. The risk of investing all that cash into infrastructure is too high. On the other hand, an Invisible Organization can expand quickly and easily. A couple of recruiters can staff a large organization in a few months and there's no capital equipment needed. A pilot program could begin within two weeks and then scale quickly from there.

An Invisible Organization can also create incredible marketing—and it should if it wants to succeed. It's how your marketing integrates with your internal systems that will make all the difference in profitability. It will allow you to fully exploit the advantages of an Invisible Organization.

In this section I will show you how you can highly optimize your marketing and take advantage of a virtual workforce that can utilize your own fully self-sustaining interconnected systems. Assuming now that you have begun to build create a strategic plan, you will soon see how you can quickly scale any sales program. You can move new staff members through your automated training environment to get them productive quickly, allowing you to expand much faster.

Later in the book I'll review how to conduct webinars, generate high quality leads with radio and TV ads, and hire people on contingency with a PEO (Professional Employers Organization.) You'll see how efficiently this can be done with almost no overhead. A PEO requires only a small monthly fee to keep staff enrolled in group insurance and payroll services, which I will cover in chapter 10.

You'll come to appreciate the way you'll be able to reconfigure divisions and departments as needed for different purposes. As your marketing changes, you can redeploy staff easily by using your automated training solutions to bring them up to speed quickly.

While I was growing my own companies, I learned so much about marketing from Jay Abraham. He taught me more about marketing in three days at one of his live events than

I'd learned in all my prior years in business. I've become a lifelong student of Jay and am enjoying every minute of it.

What Actually is Marketing?

Marketing is the art of helping prospects see the amazing value in what you offer and then leading them to an acquisition. Marketing is the creation of the entire value proposition of your company's products. It is the fuel that feeds the sales funnel. Marketing converts doubt to certainty, allowing your prospect to take the first step to acquire your product, a step which they ideally will repeat over and over again with multiple purchases.

Marketing is more than publishing ads and running commercials. If you treat it like that, your message will come across as meaningless and won't have much impact on your audience. Advertising gets the word out about your product, but by actively *listening* to what your clients have to say in return, you will develop *the art of building a relationship with your customer*. This means that marketing, in essence, is not just about increasing your business, it's about improving the lives of your clients.

Simply stated, marketing is the way we create desire on an unconscious level. It's a form of mass hypnosis. It's an art and magic that is designed to create the grandest illusion of all—to create *desire*. There is nothing more powerful than curiosity and desire. First comes the piquing of interest, making prospects curious about what it would be like to own your product and experience your service, to give them a taste of how it would *feel* to have it.

And then comes the raw, unbridled desire akin to a sexual hunger on an unconscious level. The craving is so strong your prospect *must* have it. True desire is enduring and sustaining. Before the pitch, before the close, there is something intangible and invisible to the unconscious mind like the scent of an expensive perfume that shows up before the woman does.

When great marketing is in harmony with the founder's original vision, prospects will resonate with that message and want to buy even though they may not fully understand why. *Now that's marketing!*

Marketing has changed dramatically over the years. It's almost as if a new marketing channel is being created on a daily basis. Do you remember when life was simple, when there was radio; AM and FM, TV with only thirteen channels, and newspapers and magazines? And let's not forget the Yellow Pages. In today's world marketing tools have become more and more sophisticated, but the actual purpose of marketing hasn't changed.

Harley-Davidson is a company that has tapped into one of the most powerful marketing techniques ever to rule the hearts and souls of their customers. By tapping into their prospects' belief system, they have aligned their message with who they are instead of homogenizing it to appeal to the masses.

The successful marketing campaigns of Harley-Davidson embody the true purpose of marketing—bonding with your customers on a level that transcends your product. By attracting clients in the most subtle yet powerful way through curiosity, they created an enduring desire to be a part of their brand. They have created a bond that endures quality issues, high prices and even inconvenience. The reason why customers stay loyal is because the brand is aligned with their personal identity.

When you apply the same strategy, clients will resonate with you and want to buy from you without you doing much more than showing up, because they are aligned with your vision. They want to identify with who you are, because it reminds them of who they are and resonates with it. When clients tattoo your logo on their body, you know you did it right! When you know how to wield such a powerful weapon, to create curiosity and desire in others, you can utilize the rapid scalability factor of your Invisible Organization to dominate your niche.

Yet a simple mistake or a slight shift in intention can ruin expensive campaigns. Your intention is enormously important to the outcome. For example, if the marketing director decides that a campaign should be focused on lead generation while the sales manager requested a campaign focused on lead conversion, this missed intention could waste enormous amounts of time and money. The sales manager didn't need more leads.

Social media has become a critical component of how companies create, build and control their images in the marketplace today. The Invisible Organization utilizes systems that easily connect with social media so that client feedback, no matter where and when it takes place, can be acted on quickly by your staff. Because your systems are able to listen to all social media for mention of your brand, you can respond swiftly and decisively before true brand damage is done.

Note: Internet Marketing is a critical and valuable tool you can use to drive prospects to your business, and you should. However, this is not something that this book will cover.

There's a list of suggested Internet Marketing resources on www.InvisibleOrganization.com/Resources.

Knowing Your Client Better than They Know Themselves

The more you know about your clients, the more you'll come to love and appreciate them. Your customer is the one who buys your product. This is why it's *critical* to fall in love with your clients, *not* your product.

Do you *really* know what products and services your clients need? Most business owners think they already know, but it's much better to actually *find out*. How? It's simple: just ask your clients. Your clients will give you the answers you need. You just have to learn how to ask the right questions.

Even better, when you listen to your clients' needs and wants, they will feel that you genuinely care and understand them. Once your clients see that you are responsive to their needs, they will feel you are their partner instead of a vendor. This will allow you to enter into a permission-based relationship that can provides clients with better products while creating an endless stream of new services to sell them. So find out what they want and tailor your service and products to their wishes.

Using your CRM tools, you can create a survey to get your clients input and feedback. Even if you have already done an in-depth study to learn what your customers really need and want, consider a regularly scheduled survey to check in and ask what is their biggest challenge, because nothing stays the same—including your clients' needs, the market, and your company.

The best and most creative client-based survey I've seen is from a company that asks *one* question every time a client logs in and uses their service. They don't ask their clients to fill out a long form, just one question that feeds their client profile record. Over time, this paints a detailed picture of the client's activities and their needs, which is captured in the CRM system.

Any one survey ideally should have no more than three questions. It should have one purpose and not cover a million different things. Pinpoint something specific, particularly something that the client cares about, which will help increase sales and maintain a high level of customer satisfaction.

The depth and quality of responses you'll get are much higher than you would ever get in an online survey, because over time it becomes an ongoing conversation between you and your clients. This is a great way to have a slowly evolving, deep relationship with your clients by staying in communication with them while constructing a multi-faceted, holistic picture of your client and their needs.

Your Customer By the Numbers

Your view as the leader of the business extends directly to your customers. Therefore, it's beneficial to look at them as more than just the other half of a transaction. But don't *ignore* the realities of that transaction either. You still have a business to run. So it's helpful to see your customers as partners in a *string* of transactions and repeat business.

By using the slow-survey method I described above, you are getting a clear picture of exactly who your clients are. This allows you to build a detailed customer profile or "avatar" that you will use to attract more of the same type of customers.

This can be as simple as uploading your customer list confidentially to Facebook, which you can use to build a custom audience by finding others who are just like your current customers. If you have 100 customers, Facebook will extract the common elements of those people and search all of Facebook for others with those specific elements, allowing you to find targeted prospects more easily and less expensively than before.

What is a Client Worth?

The reason to ask a question like this is to determine how much you can spend for acquiring a new customer. By digging into your past marketing expenses for a specific period of time and then comparing that to your gross sales for that same period, you can see what it costs to acquire a client.

The mistake I made as a new business owner was to compare my marketing expenses to the sales of my entry-level product. Jay Abraham introduced me to the idea of "lifetime value of a client" by helping me to see what each new client spends over time as long as they remained my customer.

This opened my eyes: I could actually lose money on my first sale as long as I would be profitable over the lifetime of the client. I had redefined the "value" of a client. I could actually spend more on marketing than I had initially thought. And I did spend more, much more, and expanded my client base quickly as more profitable clients entered into the sales funnel and stayed longer than before.

Understanding this simple concept changed everything. Now let's determine the lifetime value of your client. By carefully thinking through and answering these questions, how you look at your customers begins to shift.

1. How long do clients stay?

2. Do they continue after their initial contract expires?

3. Have they purchased additional products or services?

4. How many of your clients refer a friend or business associate?

5. What is the closing ratio of incoming leads?

6. In the last twelve months, how much have you spent on new client acquisition?

7. How much was your gross sales for that product line or group of services?

8. What is your net profit in the last twelve months for that group of clients?

There's a lot of great information from doing a simple analysis like this. A picture begins to form from the answers to these questions. Suppose the average client stays for three years, 20% continue after their initial contract expires, and 10% purchase additional products and services. For example, a company that has never really solicited referrals would obviously have zero referrals. The closing ratio on prospect meetings is about 33%.

Suppose a client stays on average for three years and generates $12,000 per year at a net profit of 20%, which would be $2,400 a year. Knowing that, how much could you spend to acquire a new client? Theoretically you could spend up to $7,200 (3 x $2,400) on marketing to get one new client and not lose money. Understanding what you really can spend frees your thinking to spend more and acquire more clients, making more profit in your business.

As Jay Abraham told me many times, the only way to increase sales is to sell more: to sell more products to new or existing clients or sell more often to existing clients.

Once you have clear answers to the questions above, you can:

- Find a way to increase the amount of time a client stays with your company.

- Add new products or services to sell to existing clients.

- Spend more money on client acquisition.

Also, as Jay explains, if you don't have new products, find someone who has products that your clients would want to buy, then sell those. Or find a new client base owned by another business and partner with them to offer your services, sharing the profits with your new partner.

I want to provide you with several ideas that will shape your future marketing efforts.

Optimizing Your Marketing Communication

The power of a stream of emails directed to prospects can, over time, have a significant positive effect. Those emails should include an invitation to connect with the company and with you as the CEO. Always encourage personal communication. If someone responds, write back immediately and make sure prospects and clients feel like their emails were read by you. The personal attention will be appreciated. Without interaction, there is no conversation, only a one-way broadcast of your thoughts and product data.

Find other ways to communicate regularly. Here are a few ideas:

- Send a welcome email to new clients, asking them to click a link and answer a few questions that will allow you to serve them better. Capture their answers in your CRM system and use their own words in your campaigns.

- Interview an expert in the industry or have existing clients ask you questions that will allow prospects to see what you do and what you offer. Invite your clients and prospects to listen and ask questions at the end. This encourages more interaction and showcases your company products and services while building a more personal connection with your clients.

- Host weekly webinars free of charge that teach your clients to better use your products. Even though they are free, you can promote higher-level paid webinars to deliver specialized information or train clients to take their own business even further.

- Organize a live event where you "disclose all your se-crets"— what you've done, how you did it, and what it takes to be successful in your field. Explain that the event will be a transformational shift in how they view them-selves and their own business. Promise something big and let them leave with a plan!

- Set aside one hour a week at the same time and day called, "Ask the CEO," when you take incoming calls personally. This is a huge boost to your image, and clients love it!

- Record all calls, events, teleseminars and webinars. Then package them and create a series of products you can sell.

- Write a book. A book establishes your credibility and expands your reputation as an authority. Then you can provide a free book to all clients who take some sort of action. (To find resources that will help you write and publish your own book, go to www.InvisibleOrganization.com/Resources.)

I bet you can implement one or more of these tactics to better communicate who you are to your clients, forge a closer relationship with them, and generate more business.

Go out and start that dialogue. Watch how powerful the results will be!

Remember, marketing is *the art of building a relationship with your prospects and then your customers.* That relationship starts with the first contact and continues for as long as you are invited into their inbox with valuable information they enjoy receiving.

By feeding your prospects relevant marketing data, tips, tutorials and industry news, and by regularly interacting with your clients, you'll be able to strengthen your relationships, which promotes loyalty. Clients expect you to get to know them, they want to hear more about what *they* need, not what *you* want to sell. Find out what they need and make it happen for them.

9

A Unique Selling and Relationship Machine

When used correctly, webinars are an amazing tool that can pay off big time! When you carefully define the goal and purpose of your webinars in advance, you can turn it into a closing machine. The technology makes it all work seamlessly, and it doesn't matter where the presenter is. The webinars are conducted in a web meeting room, your clients are at their homes or offices anywhere in the world, and all the information about attendees is tracked and recorded in the CRM system. In an Invisible Organization where we strive to operate from a unified database, the path from prospect to webinar attendee to client should require entering prospect information only once.

Since there are people who have a negative idea about webinars, come up with a name that will make it more appealing for your prospects and clients to attend. We called our webinar "Master Class," which was exactly what it was. The webinar is just the medium. Highlight the topic and make it enticing by focusing on the benefits they will get from attending. The key to hosting successful webinars is providing every attendee with a highly positive experience, a transformation if possible, that shows a new and better way of doing something.

In my last company, we made our webinars highly interactive. Before the webinar, every attendee was asked to fill out an extensive questionnaire to insure they would participate at the highest level. This worked well, and most people came prepared. Our goal was to create a true transformation in the lives of our clients during the webinar. We did this by making the attendees work actively. We not only showed clients how to create their own business plans, we made them work on it live during the webinar guided by the presenter and the help of other CEOs who attended.

Webinars are also a great tool to train staff or educate your clients on how to do something specific. These webinars are low pressure since selling is not the goal. They may be less interactive yet very effective at accomplishing the goal, which is to train clients and staff. When you record these webinars, they can be used as part of your virtual training environment (which we covered in chapter six).

Webinar technology has advanced quickly, and by the time you read this, it will likely have advanced even more. A simple tool that does the job is "Go to Webinar." It is relatively inexpensive. The downside is that it doesn't connect readily into other systems, which we strive to accomplish.

Another now popular webinar system is called WebinarJam. com which is low cost and can accommodate an unlimited number of attendees.

There are webinar systems that do connect directly to several CRM systems, and one of them is Omnovia. Omnovia can be integrated with your CRM system, deliver useful information to your presenter as he or she manages attendees in the web room, and effectively employs live video. Some webinar systems give you the ability to measure participation, present interactive testing, and have small group break-outs in the same webinar environment.

As new technology continues to emerge, check the resource page www.InvisibleOrganization.com/Resources for the most updated recommendation.

The Sales Webinar

Selling a high-priced product to a new prospect is hard. A prospect usually has a learning curve before he's fully comfortable with risking investment in a multi-thousand dollar product. A webinar is the most perfect tool to build trust with your clients and educate them on why making such a big investment is the best thing to do.

Webinars can become the "entry ramp" for prospects to enter your world. The effort to make them as powerful and valuable as possible will pay big dividends. The best way to sell anything is to make your prospects believe that they need what you have to offer. Most of the time, people have a need but can't truly identify how to satisfy that need.

Here's an example: we used radio and TV ads to attract our target clients. When a prospect called our 800-number, we sold them a low-cost master class on how to create a business road map for higher profits and faster growth. Our virtual sales staff was equipped with a carefully designed and polished sales script. (Those who followed the script closed the most business. The more "creative" sales reps became, the less they sold. Scripting is an art, and it takes years of experience to master this art.)

We always offered an "iron-clad" money-back guarantee. If prospects attended the webinar and didn't believe we provided them with massive value as we promised, we would refund their money. We had very few requests for refunds, and because we removed the risk, we were able to share our brilliance with more people. Using the money back guarantee, a Jay Abraham risk reversal strategy, those "on the fence" could experience our training risk-free.

In an Invisible Organization, selling must be frictionless just like everything else. Your salespeople must be able to close quickly and efficiently. The only way to do that is to eliminate all administrative duties as much as possible so that your sales reps can focus completely on prospects and closing sales.

Closing Sales in the Webinar Environment

From my experience selling high-priced products using webinars, you'll have the highest conversion ratio by delivering massive value up front and showing prospects what next step they can take to build on the gains they received from the first webinar.

The master presenters I've seen who closed substantial business in a webinar environment bonded with the attendees, building a personal relationship with them. They involved the attendees in the processes of creating something of high value and led them through the exercises to achieve that. Because the attendees realized that they needed the information that was being taught, the closing ratio was very high. The credibility of the presenter plays a very important role. Why would anyone believe a presenter who never accomplished the end results of the course he's teaching?

The Value Strategy

Once clients had paid $229 for their seat in our webinar, we wanted them to receive massive value and be convinced they did. Our goal was twofold:

1. Keep the webinar sold so we wouldn't have to refund their money

2. Expose them to a vastly more comprehensive system that would change their lives if acquired and implemented

After about two hours into the three-hour webinar, we asked the attendees how much value they had received up to that point. They would tell us that it was worth anywhere from $10,000 up to $2,000,000. We would ask them to write down this number *before* we attempted to close the *big* sale, the reason we conducted the webinar in the first place. Can you see how compelling we made our multi-thousand-dollar product? Attendees could only imagine that if they were given over $10,000 in value for just $229, what an incredible value they would get if they were to invest $4,000 in the high-end product.

Pitch, Sell, Deliver

Some people will have buyer's remorse and may want to return the product even before they've experienced its benefits. Obviously, the faster you can get the product into their hands, the less chance of buyer's remorse you'll have to deal with. In the past, we shipped a twenty-five-pound box filled with work books, DVDs and CDs, even an MP3 player filled with the content of the CDs. The package took a week to arrive. As you can imagine, we experienced several returns before the client even received the box. That is why I highly recommend using electronic delivery for immediate access. If there is a physical component, deliver it later. Get the product in their hands as quickly as possible and everyone is happier.

Making a Free Webinar Work

Free has often been equated with valueless, and in many cases it's true. The old saying warns, "If it looks too good to be true, it probably is." Prospects assume that most free webinars are going to be sales pitches with no "real" value. That's why free webinars have such a low show-up rate.

Another downfall of free webinars is that your attendees are mostly broke. Yup, they won't buy because they can't. Even if you wow them to the point of tears, it won't matter if they don't have the funds to take the next step. We've proven this over and over to the point that some attendees actually requested their money back, forgetting it was free.

Since we sold to business owners, a simple way to tell if a client would be viable was how successful their business was... or wasn't. In our paid webinar series we tried to determine if a prospect would be worth pursuing by asking them how big their current business was. We quickly realized that dreamers and those at the very beginning stages of planning a new business can't afford much.

My suggestion is to avoid free webinars unless you host a recorded webinar and automate it. The conversion rate may be low, but so will your cost be. While content is still the most important thing to develop, the offer and method of delivery will make a huge difference to your success. A pre-recorded webinar that directs to a buy page has to be so strong, so compelling that it closes by itself.

Maybe you've received a telephone call from a machine pitching one thing or another. Most likely you hung up before it even started. Amazingly, you receive those calls because they work. Enough people hold on after the call ends to be connected to a live agent who closes the transaction. The same thing goes for an automated webinar. Since it costs pennies to run each time, even if one person is listening, it closes enough to *sometimes* justify its use.

However, even with automated webinars where costs are low, you still need to generate leads that will create the audience for these automated webinars. A lead costs money, and sometimes automated webinars simply don't close enough to justify the cost of leads. Perhaps you could use automated webinars for dead leads, those who inquired but never purchased. What do you have to lose? The leads are virtually free since you already purchased them.

I don't discuss these systems in this book, but we've set those systems up for clients and would be happy to discuss how you might make use of them in your own organization. Contact me at mitch@invisibleorganization.com.

10

Crushing Your Competition: Recruiting Superstars

Revenue is the lifeblood of a business. Without sales, there is no business. Therefore, selecting the best people is crucial and in many cases the "x factor" that makes a company most successful in its niche.

Most companies don't have dozens of salespeople sitting in cubicles scattered within a leased office building. When CEOs consider selling their products with live salespeople, they might consider it prohibitive to build a new physical call center and populate it with trained sales reps. If you are that CEO and you want to create that sales floor, you will need sales managers roaming the cubicles listening to pitches, answering questions, and helping out if needed. Because the expense is so high, many companies turn to call centers. Call centers are great if you have simple information that needs to be collected from callers, but they generally don't work well when a complex sales process is required.

It's a paradox, since you need salespeople. Without a qualified, trained, and tested sales team, your company cannot grow. But you don't want to hire them and build a sales floor, yet you also realize that you risk poor results if you hire a call center.

The solution is to hire your own salespeople and deploy them as a virtual team.

In an Invisible Organization, everything is done with much greater speed and efficiency. There's no leased office space, no cubicles, no in-house PBX, no phone equipment, no parking lot, no snow days, no sick days, and no big salaries. You're running an Invisible Organization, and those things are ancient relics of the past.

What's more, your sales team is the best in the business: they are highly trained, all with the exact same powerful materials, all thoroughly tested to insure they will succeed, and all anxious to work from home. If you hire a sales team with staying power, they will produce results over and over again like clockwork. Because you are operating virtually, you must have greater control through systems so your management can quickly enhance areas of weakness or cut people who are not performing.

In your Invisible Organization, your sales manager is potentially "watching" hundreds of salespeople logged into the call center system and is monitoring every aspect of their performance. Besides being able to silently barge in and listen to calls, he can see who is closing at the highest rate, who is wasting leads, and who is taking a lot of breaks. The console gives more insight into the actual work habits of your staff than managers wandering the sales floor could ever give you.

You want to streamline your sales process so that you are operating efficiently and producing the greatest revenue yield. Having Sales Superstars is critically important to the success of your Invisible Organization.

This chapter will teach you how to screen, select and train a team of Sales Superstars.

Chet Holmes introduced me to the concept of *The Superstar*, and thanks to working with him and his companies, I've fine-tuned my own sales staffing philosophy. Over the years prior to working with Chet, I had run several sales teams. Once in a while a "superstar" would show up, hit the ball out of the park in the first few weeks, but then appear at the bottom of the list a couple months later. He succumbed to failure and didn't fight back. Now that I know how to screen for real Sales Superstars, I've been able to hire many of them who have continued to be top producers for years.

Real Sales Superstars are game changers. Their internal desire to succeed is what inspires them to win. They are wired to thrive on rejection. They don't conform to their environment but instead overcome it, setting new records nearly every month by fully committing themselves to training, reading, practicing, listening to past sales calls, and mirroring other successful salespeople. They know failure is not who they are. Those who succeed have learned to see sales as a numbers game: it's simple math. Twenty-three "no's" in a row isn't fun, but those who understand the game won't let it stop them.

When I sold for a living as a young man, I had to make a hundred calls just to make one sale. At first I felt discouraged, but once I realized that I was actually getting paid $100 for every "no" because each sale was worth $10,000, my attitude changed. I was no longer "failing." My results were very predictable. That simple reframing made all the difference in the world. The highs and lows began to dissipate as I became emotionally detached from the outcome. To some degree, you can test for that psychological aspect in someone's personality. I'll show you what to look for and how to find it.

We use a specially designed test to confirm if we have actually located a true Sales Superstar. Go to www.InvisibleOrganization.com/Resources for instructions on how to take the assessment yourself or set up assessments for candidates.

What is the Definition of a Sales Superstar?

Sales Superstars have that elusive quality of superior selling skills combined with persistence, intelligence, and confidence. You can put them in a bad situation and they excel anyway. A Sales Superstar performs under *any* conditions and outsells his peers by 200-500%. Even when given poor training, bad tools and old leads, they'll still come out on top.

The core discovery that Chet made is this: the best salespeople have that perfect balance of ego and empathy. Too much ego and the rep will always try to close but never build a relationship with a prospect. Too much empathy and the rep will build a warm relationship with his prospect but never close.

It's that delicate balance of ego strength and empathy that makes the difference. You want to find that *ideal* individual who can build relationships and close sales. Sales Superstars work well in teams because they easily convince others of their viewpoint and are excellent communicators.

Adding just one true Sales Superstar to your team will raise the bar for the entire team. Unless you build a system to guide you and your recruiters through each step of the process, however, it's nearly impossible to find that person.

Getting the Best People in the World to Work for You

Knowing how to build and lead a great team virtually makes it possible to attract the very best people in the entire country—and even the world. If you stay local, you might find only the best people in your city. Which one would you rather have?

But before you place an ad, you must ask yourself a very important question: "What type of person am I looking for?" Are you looking for a "closer" or an "appointment setter" or someone who can do both? Prospecting and selling obviously require different skills and personality types. If you hire a salesperson, he should be focused on selling. If you hire a prospector, then his job is to set appointments.

Sales can be *incredibly* difficult, especially if there's cold calling involved. It can be demoralizing and soul crushing if cold calling is relegated to a professional salesperson. Great salespeople shouldn't be wasted on cold calling. One of the most cost effective ways to fully utilize your sales talent is to hire appointment setters who simply warm up the prospect first and set appointments for your Sales Superstars.

Great appointment setters contribute to the success and longevity of the Sales Superstars at your company. Appointment setters get paid a small base salary and a tiny incentive when a sale from one of their leads closes. How do you find a great appointment setter?

I suggest placing an ad in the paper that says:

Would you like to make money talking on the phone? All you have to do is call prospects and arrange an appointment with one of our salespeople. We'll pay you $12 an hour, plus you'll receive a $100 bonus for every closed sale.

Just take a moment to think about this. We've had a rough economy for a number of years, which means there are people struggling to find work. There are millions of unemployed people and plenty of individuals who want a career change or the opportunity to earn a higher income.

By having clearly defined roles, you can build a stronger team. Companies who utilize this strategy help their Sales Superstars reach much higher levels of performance.

Learning how to attract and screen the right candidate can change the lives of everyone in your company. By adding the highest quality people you'll raise the bar for everybody else, which increases the performance of the team and makes everybody more money.

You need to reject people quickly and see if they bounce back. If they do, you have the chance to take them to the next phase of the interview process. Once you've hired them, you have to have a highly efficient system in place to properly train them and continually motivate them to perform at a high level, as we've previously discussed.

To draw Sales Superstars, you need compelling ads that do the heavy lifting. Remember that a true Sales Superstar is someone who has the perfect balance between ego strength (closing) and empathy (bonding) and is driven to succeed. True Sales Superstars are not going to give up, they don't stop until they win, they make progress where others don't, and they love to make money.

Instead of trying to get a lot of responses, you want to attract candidates who fit the profile and are challenged by rejection. Your ad could be:

Sales Superstar wanted!

Potential to earn between $50,000 and $300,000 annually. Don't even apply unless you are the best at what you do.

An ad like this will scare weak candidates away and will grab the attention of those who have a strong self-image and are extremely focused on making money in sales. Some unfit people will still apply, but you'll screen them out quickly. You can use Craigslist, Monster.com or the local job boards. As long as you get the ad right, you'll have success.

Place the ad in several places and see what responses you get. At the end of the ad, send candidates to a landing page that explains the position from top to bottom. Provide details regarding the entire pay structure including any benefits or perks. The landing page is not just to provide information about the job—it's also designed to screen the candidates and cut out weak personalities.

Be blunt and dissuade people from applying unless they are at the top of their field. Statements like this are useful: "If you are not in the top 5% of applicants for this position, save your time and do not apply." The landing page should fully educate the candidate on the position. If they are selected for an interview, you can maintain complete control of the interview process. If someone says, "So tell me more about the position," you know he didn't read the landing page and he has already disqualified himself.

Interview Strategies that Landed Me a Company Filled with Top Producers

After hiring hundreds of sales executives personally, I can assure you that a person with the right personality profile will outsell an average salesperson who has been through a good training program any day of the month. I fine-tuned the process Chet taught me to hire and train top sales professionals for all our clients and all my own companies. What were the results? We were staffed with top Sales Superstars across all our divisions who tested high, delivered consistent results, and stayed with us for years.

Obviously, your Sales Superstar needs to make a strong first impression. There's no better chance for this than during his first interview. The first interview is short. After introducing yourself briefly, spend less than five minutes on general dialogue like, "How about the Red Sox?" or "I hear the weather in Seattle is pretty bad this month." Then get down to business. Your first question should be, "The ad said we are looking for Sales Superstars only. What makes you think you are a Sales Superstar?" Start off nice. Then be tough and observe his (or her) reaction. He may not know how to respond. Whatever he says, respond with, "Well, I am not hearing Superstar."[2] And just be quiet.

One of two things will happen. He'll say, "Okay, thanks," and hang up. Or he'll say something like, "Well, as I just explained, I was top producer at XYZ, and I won the 2012 Salesman of the Year Award." This is good. You have a possible candidate. At that point, explain that you have a large candidate pool and while he might have succeeded in the past, this job is very challenging. Once again, you want him to reassure you that he is at the top of his game. You want his ego's strength to shine. If he's the right person, he'll want to win. Losing even an interview is unacceptable. He should push politely but firmly. If he does, reluctantly agree to a second interview.

By asking the right questions you'll conduct interviews in a way that will reveal the strongest and weakest attributes of the candidate. You test how a candidate reacts to a similar environment as a selling situation. The psychological profile is the secret to determine whether you are talking with a

---

2   Note: Be prepared to get complaints. It has happened before. People don't like to get rejected even if they are simply being told they are not sales material. Let it go… and have your assistant screen your calls.

Sales Superstar. They have two distinct personality traits as determined by the DISC (Dominance, Influence, Steadiness, Conscientiousness) personality testing system.

- They are high dominant: they get things done and are respected by their peers.

- They are high influence: they are naturally empathetic and love to be with people.

The second interview is more in-depth. Less than 10% of those who applied will make it to the next round. If the percentage is much higher, you weren't firm enough. In the beginning you might be concerned how you make the candidate feel. Remember, though, that you're not doing yourself or the candidate a favor by being nice or giving them a break. It will be a waste of time and money. Eventually they *will* fail, but not after you've invested in training, spent time integrating them into your company, and paid them a draw on future commissions that they'll never earn. *Be firm.* Follow the process, and you'll both get what you need.

The basic premise of this interview technique is based on Chet's three main points:

Relax, Probe and Attack.

Your first goal is to let your candidate relax and show his best side. Let him talk about his successes in life, his passions in life, and his best personal traits. You really want him to relax and drop his guard. In your short interview, you were gruff and business-like. Now as you start your long interview process, your switch to Mr. or Ms. Nice may come as a surprise. Skip questions about age, race, religion, or anything that could discriminate in any way.

Check with your H/R department or legal counsel if needed. If you get permission up front from your candidate to ask questions about his life and explain that he doesn't have to answer, you should be ok. Explain that you're using a personality profiling system to see if he's a fit.

Start with a question like, "Would you agree that *who* you are is more important than what you've *done*?" If he says, "Yes," your next statement could be, "I agree. Now I'd like to ask you about your childhood. Would you be okay with that?" If he says, "Yes," you have a green light to proceed. If he says, "No," find out why. Remind him that he can refuse to answer any question that makes him uncomfortable, but refusing or being uncomfortable is a sign he's not really empathetic.

He should *want* to share and show you who he is. If at any point the candidate is not empathetic or gets hostile, you're done. If he's dishonest, you're done. Chet Holmes explains more in his book *The Ultimate Sales Machine*. (Get his book and study chapter five. Everything is there. It's worth the investment.)

Now, it's time to... *Attack!*

This is where you get to see what he is really made of. Can he stand up to the rejection he'll face on the phone? The process is carefully designed to test his strength against rejection. You can transition from *Relax* to *Attack* by saying, "Thank you for sharing so much about your life. After hearing your story, I'm sure you're a good person, but I don't think you have what it takes to make it in our company." *Now.... Shut Up!* Just listen to what happens next. The whole interview has been designed for this moment of truth.

One time I was screening candidates for a sales manager position with a clothing company based in New York. A woman made it through the first interview with ease. She had ample experience in the fashion business, had run a sales force in the past, and had grown several product lines using many different marketing techniques. We bonded quickly in the second interview. I admired her warmth and ability to get comfortable talking. I smiled as she spoke. I was in recruiting heaven. I thought I had found the perfect candidate.

After I told her, "You don't have what it takes," I shut up and let her respond. She said, "Okay, thank you," and hung up. I was shocked! I couldn't believe she caved, but she did. And I didn't call back. I wanted to, but it would've been of no value to anyone if I had. No matter how impressive her track record was, she was *not* a Sales Superstar: she caved under the smallest amount of pressure.

This story illustrates just how important this screening process is and *how well it works*. At times I've given candidates "one more chance," and it has always backfired. Applicants with stellar resumes and broad work experience who can't make it through this intensive screening aren't going to be successful. If you let them through, they'll be unhappy, get sick, or feel they don't fit in because they have to try so hard just to keep up. It really is best for both parties that you don't hire people who don't have the right personality for the position.

During the interview process you are rejecting the candidate to test his "ego strength." Understand that the best candidates will try to get the job while the worst candidates want you to convince them why they would want to work for your company.

"I want the job! What do I have to do to get it?" asked the young man on the other end of the phone. "I'm sorry, but I am just not hearing Superstar, and my ad specifically stated we are looking for Sales Superstars." There was an uncomfortable silence.

I was waiting for what happened next. "Ok," he said. "Let's review. I was the number one salesperson on a team of thirty-six and had double the sales of the salesperson before me. In a prior company, I was number four in a team of 500 reps who all had more experience than me. In my first sales position, I outsold 495 of them in just six months. What else do I need to do to convince you that you have the best possible candidate on the phone with you right now?"

I smiled and thought, "This is my guy." Instead of telling him what I was thinking I said, "Ok. Here's what I can do. We have several killer candidates for this position, and I'm looking for the best. I'd be willing to give you thirty days to prove yourself. Whoever has the highest sales at the end of the thirty days gets the job. You need to understand that there's no base pay. There are no benefits unless you get hired, but there is a great upside for the one who performs." Once again.... there was total silence on my part. His next words were, "When do I start?" By drawing out the ego strength in your candidate you can test how strong his drive is.

Sometimes people are driven to do well during an interview, but they don't perform on the job. This interview process is just one part of a multi-step system that will later test their ability to present and perform well under pressure.

Sales Superstars are rare. You have to search carefully to find them. They show up in the oddest places. And I have to warn you, Sales Superstars aren't the easiest people to manage. They can be demanding, temperamental, and self-centered. They *should* be. Those traits go with the territory. But don't be easily fooled—those characteristics don't automatically mean someone is a Sales Superstar.

Since most of the interview process is done over the phone, you'll know what your candidate will sound like to prospects. This is one part of screening your candidates. Sales requires charisma and good presentation skills, so it only makes sense to do your final interviews over Skype and see what your candidate looks like. In many cases you will get clues to their environment as well, such as a cluttered space or animals that roam freely within their workspace.

If they present well, use a screen-sharing program like GoToMeeting.com and have them enter a lead on your system while you watch. A great salesman who can't enter an order (operate your technology) is not going to last more than a day. This tests how well they will do in your training environment and exposes computer illiteracy quickly. Don't skip this last step. I can't tell you how many staff we've hired who sounded great and passed all our tests but couldn't comfortably handle simple tasks on their computer.

You will soon discover, by observing how diligently they get through the training, how well they will work in a virtual environment. That's how you judge their ability to focus. Once they are hired, your virtual call center will track every move they make, and your sales manager can set alerts to indicate inactivity.

Structuring Compensation for Maximum Results

- How do you determine the pay structure?

- Should you pay a draw against commission?

- Should you pay a training bonus?

- A base salary?

Let's explore possible answers to these questions. When building a pay plan, this is the key question: how many days does it take before someone can make money working solely on commission? Assuming they have made it through your Sales Superstar screening process, you are ready to pitch them on taking the job. If they can make money in a week, you just have to make sure they are well trained. After you hire them, give them a little cash up-front and call it a "training bonus." You'll know in a week or two whether or not they're going to be successful.

Earlier I shared with you that it took me 100 calls to make one $10,000 sale. It was predictable. A productive person could make 100 calls in a day or so. This could give you a basis for how long it should take a new person to make money.

Usually those with families and obligations cannot take as much risk as younger folks who have low overhead and few obligations. This doesn't mean they are out of the picture. Instead, this means they need to be brought on board in a different way.

What do you do if it takes months for a new salesperson to make money? Here's a scenario from a client I worked with:

- It takes two months of training to bring a new Sales Superstar up to speed.

- Then it could take another two months to build a pipeline of prospects.

- In the fifth month, he should close his first sale.

You can't expect someone to go without being paid for five months. Imagine the conversation over dinner that night: "Hey, honey, I got a new job!" His wife responds with excitement: "Congratulations! That is great! How much does it pay?" And he has to answer, "Well, nothing for the first 5 months..." How do you think that conversation will end?

It's very important that you recruit the right person since there is always a startup investment. If the candidate made it through the Sales Superstar hiring process, the probability of success is very high. It's likely worth paying him a training bonus of $2,000 a month (more or less) for the first three months depending on the cost of living in his area. Then transition him to a draw against commission.

You can explain that in month three, you'll pay $3,000 a month "draw against commission," which means that you are giving him a loan on future earnings that he'll have to repay. Then once he starts earning commissions, $1,000 per month will be deducted from his pay until he has paid it back. It would be advisable to limit the draw to three months after the first month of training.

You could push your new salesperson to be more aggressive and close faster by using a percentage of his commission and draw amounts as a motivator. Let's say you can afford to pay 12% commission. Reduce it by 2% when you propose your pay plan and use that extra 2% to accelerate your salesperson's progress in closing his first sale. Offer to increase his commission by 1% permanently for each month if he doesn't need a draw against commission for that additional month.

In other words, if he decides that after the first two months of training he only needs one month of draw against commission instead of three he can earn 12% commission permanently instead of the normal 10%. This means that by foregoing two months of draw, he is awarded a higher commission rate for being more entrepreneurial. You can let him decide after his training. It will tell you a lot about your new hire. If he is aggressive and trims two months from his draw, everyone wins. This example is complex and works best with a long sales cycle.

Most companies don't have a long sales cycle. With shorter sales cycles, you put the new rep through a few weeks of training and get him started. If you run a company where a telesales rep reads the script and can close in fifteen minutes, he can start making money fairly quickly and your commission plan can be simple. You might only provide a small training bonus. But after that, compensation should be based on performance.

Adjust these ideas based on the length of your sales cycle and complexity of your product line. Overall, you want to use your pay structure to create a highly incentivized environment that will get you the best results. If your new salesperson doesn't step up and show results after a reasonable time frame, you need to let him go. Take your loses and move on.

Slashing Salaries and Boosting Compensation for Your Top Tier

Often when CEOs take a close look at their sales force they find that some salespeople are doing incredibly well while others are not even generating enough revenue to cover their base salary. And to make matters worse, every member of the sales team is getting paid the same salary. A better strategy is to significantly reduce base salaries and raise the commission. Pay for health insurance costs and taxes to stay completely legal, but beyond that your people need to get paid what they are worth.

You may lose some folks at the lower end of the performance scale, but those at the top will earn more than before. That's perfect! They become the example for everyone else. I've worked with companies where 80% of the compensation is paid as salary and the balance is paid on performance through commissions. My advice is to reverse that. Drop your paid salary to about 20% and raise commission on the per-sale basis to reach a total of 80%. The commission checks that you'll be writing to your top performers will be much higher, your lower end staff will drop off, and that makes room for more Sales Superstars.

There is a formula that you can use to determine how to set up an incentive-based compensation plan. It's not a precise mathematical formula. It's more of a guideline based on some variables which are illustrated below:

1. How long does it take to close a sale?

2. What is the value of each sale closed?

3. What percentage of the sale can you pay to the salesperson[3]?

4. How many sales does your best salesperson close in one month?

5. What is that person's closing percentage?

6. Are there follow-on sales that allow the original salesperson to make additional money?

7. What percentage of those who buy, buy something else?

8. How many months are there between the first and the second sale?

---

3 When calculating what percentage of the sale you can pay a salesperson, keep in mind the lifetime value of a customer. In other words, if you make a sale to a customer, how much more will this customer spend with you in his lifetime? If it's $5,000, then in theory you can pay your salesman more than if it were just that one $300 sale. In fact, you could give away the entire $300 to the salesperson and still be ahead of the game. That's not recommended since you likely want to try and cover some promotional costs.

9. How many months does it take to train a new recruit?

10. What are the average living expenses where your sales rep lives?

Now let's construct a pay plan based on the information provided:

1. The sale is a telephone sale and takes fifteen minutes to close. The sales rep will earn commissions in his first month.

2. The value of each sale is $300.

3. The sales commission is $125.

4. The best salesperson closes sixteen sales a month, about four per week.

5. The best salesperson's closing rate is 10% on the first call.

6. The next purchase his client makes earns the salesperson another $125 for each follow-on sale made. So the potential for each sale is about $250 per sale, but on average it's $187.50 per sale by the second month, taking into account that not everyone buys the second item.

7. We know that about 50% of those sold buy a second time.

8. This next sale usually happens within two months.

9. It takes less than a month for a new sales rep to be trained and make his first sale.

10. Our sales rep lives in a neighborhood outside New Orleans in a semi-rural area and requires just a few thousand dollars to cover his basic living expenses on a monthly basis.

Here's how that compensation plan looks:

Four sales per week	$500
Two follow-on sales per week	$250
Total income for the week	$750

Here's how to present this to the candidate:

"Our current best salesperson makes about $37,500 a year. That's without the occasional incentives and spiffs (bonuses) we frequently offer to the sales force to motivate them. Based on your background, you should be able to do better. You'll have to work hard, but you'll get paid very well." The candidate's confidence will shine through assuring you that he will do at least as well if not better than your best salesperson.

The compensation can be structured in many different ways. I once had a client who wanted to hire a Sales Superstar to sell their payday loan services. I had two great candidates, but the client didn't want to pay a training bonus twice. So I told each candidate, "I believe you are an excellent candidate for the job, but I have another candidate that is just as good, possibly even better than you. I have an idea. I already ran it by the other candidate, and she accepted." I followed with the proposition, "How about I split the training bonus with you both? Instead of $2,000 per month, we'll pay you $1,000 each, and in thirty days we'll know who is the best."

He immediately took the challenge, anxious to prove he was a Sales Superstar, and said, "If your other candidate is willing to do that, I am, too." Now I had two Sales Superstars who started working immediately, and my client didn't have to spend extra money. It turned out they were both excellent— and both were hired!

Training your Sales Superstars

In chapter six, I covered the importance of automated training environments to guarantee the quality of your team's message and to monitor each virtual rep's progress. New candidates will show their strengths and weaknesses in the area of discipline. If they can't get through the materials and dedicate time every day to learning the skills required for their new position, odds are they won't do well in the long run.

In order for your sales team to succeed, you must develop high quality sales training and be able to repeat it over and over with new hires and new supervisors. You want to train people well enough to sell your product but not over-train them. How much information will your salespeople need to know before they can sell your product or service? What materials will they need? Most of the time new salespeople are overeducated and are taught more than they need to know to close the sale.

The goal is to arm the sales team with the differentiating information that sets them apart from the competition. You'll never train a salesperson to say things the way you say them unless you use technology to impart the details of what you are selling. That's why using an automated training system deployed over the web is an essential component to creating and duplicating highly trained, high performance salespeople.

TO use automated training tools, create a list of all the steps required to take a salesperson from "just hired" to "ready to work" no matter what the assigned training materials are—chapters in a book, a Power Point presentation, a video, or a series of recorded phone calls for training purposes. Now you have "encapsulated" the training process.

You should design a test in your virtual training environment to determine if your salespeople have studied the material and completed the training. During their training you'll be able to track their progress and see how quickly they move through the materials (as explained in chapter six).

A well-trained Sales Superstar will be up to speed quickly and make more money faster. Your Invisible Organization will benefit from the increased revenue. Every salesperson will be trained to follow the carefully crafted sales script and handle objections the same way.

After they have completed the automated training process, allow them to listen in on live calls, matching them with your best salespeople. This way they will connect the reality of their new job with the material they studied. At the end of this process, there's a wrap-up interview. Check to see if they're still excited and confident that they can close sales.

The next step is to get them started using leads from the database. Make sure you have all calls recorded. Their manager should make sure they handle the calls professionally, stick to the script, and deal with objections as trained. In order to keep the job they have to close a certain number of sales within a specific time frame.

We used older leads from our database for this part of the training. At this point—after passing all the tests, drilling with a manager or a senior staff member, and meeting their first sales target—they have proven they can do the job and are officially welcomed to the team.

To provide new sales staff with ongoing support, you can assign them to experienced sales executives. This mentor/protégé relationship will not only help the new sales rep, it will tell you who your next generation managers are—those who make their protégés succeed. Of course, they are compensated for being a mentor with a commission split: the mentor gets 25% of the protégé's commission while in training. This way there's a financial incentive for the extra time and effort they invest.

After the initial training, you want to continue instilling in your salespeople a sense of excitement about their potential to make lots of money. You want to remind them that based on their performance they will be compensated very well. In an Invisible Organization, you are not likely to meet your staff members in person, since your team may live anywhere in the world. Therefore it's even more important to keep them motivated.

The personality of your sales manager will be the single

greatest factor in keeping your sales team performing. He can use tools like a spiff calendar, an incentive-based contest designed to drive salespeople to their highest level of achievement.

There are different types of spiffs. A bad spiff is one in which too many people hit the sales target (whether this is a number of sales or a specific dollar amount,) in a short period of time. Or, the opposite where only one person hits the target. The contest is over and everyone else loses. A good spiff provides a chance for everyone to win and rewards stepping up and performing beyond their previous levels.

Examples of good spiffs we've used are:

- Anyone who exceeded their last highest month by at least 10% received an extra 2% commission for that whole month. (Assuming lead flow is constant and seasonality is not a factor.)

- Anyone who closed at least seven sales received a $50 dining gift card. (Five sales was the average.)

- Anyone who exceeded their sales consistently by 5% for four consecutive months received a three-day vacation certificate (available online inexpensively) and $200 cash to enjoy their vacation.

Some more great ideas are:

- Give two tickets to Tony Robbins' incredible event *Unleash the Power Within* if they rank within the top 40% of the team for the next X months. They will have to cover their own expenses, but the ticket is generally $500.

- Give away an iPad for the top three salespeople this month.

- Treat the entire team to pizza if they achieve the team goal. (You can arrange with a major chain to deliver the pizza to their houses.)

- Give them a Starbucks or Dunkin' Donuts gift card for every sale over their average.

- Commit to donate to a charity. Once our incredible Sales Vice President Rosina Fischer committed to personally donate $500 to a good cause, and the company agreed to match her donation if the team hit a certain number of sales. She motivated the entire team to perform even beyond their own expectations, in part because they wanted to please her, generate a positive outcome in the world, and of course make more money. It worked superbly!

As you can see, there are many different ways to motivate the sales team in an Invisible Organization without having to see them in your building every day. Obviously these same techniques work well in a physical call center, too.

Be creative, be enthusiastic, and let people win often. That's how you succeed!

The Elite Sales Superstars

A key secret to encourage peak performance of your Sales Superstars is to select a privileged few to *The Inner Circle*, a sub-team of the best-of-the-best sales reps. It's the perfect way to groom your best Sales Superstars and make them advance in earnings and status. They are rewarded with extra training, free products, special exclusive activities, and they are given the opportunity to be promoted to higher posts.

Having one or two good months doesn't get someone into The Inner Circle. It should require a series of high achievements and advanced training programs to qualify. All promotions to leadership positions should come from The Inner Circle. This way everyone will be motivated to become part of it.

In my last company, I personally met with The Inner Circle members weekly and did performance coaching just for that elite group. After each coaching session, their sales increased. Afterwards I would hear how much they loved the connection with me as the CEO and how special it made them feel.

Assigning The Inner Circle members to special projects is another way to reward them. When I built a new team designed to handle a specific type of client, we selected members from The Inner Circle to staff that team. The Inner Circle will be your core team that will stay with your company for the longest time. Logically the highest paid salespeople should be The Inner Circle members.

The Bane of All Teams: Meetings

Salespeople hate meetings, yet meetings are too important to skip. Whereas some CEOs want to meet too frequently, others don't meet often enough. It's important that the CEO's time is focused on growing the business, not running it. That's what management is for. Your job as the CEO is to balance the time you spend with your sales team with the time spent with your management team, keeping your involvement a privileged, rare, and special thing, when you have a larger organization. With smaller organizations, constant and regular contact with the CEO is not unusual.

The sales team should meet three times per week for training, announcements and review. One of these meetings can be up to an hour while the other two may last just thirty minutes. The one-hour meeting should include the entire sales team, management, and the Vice President or CEO for roleplaying. Previously recorded sales calls, both good and bad, can be used as examples in these training meetings. If presented correctly, even reps who have bad calls will be grateful for the coaching. When a rep is "tuned up" by the CEO or VP, his sales should immediately increase. He should actually consider himself lucky because of the personal attention he has received to improve his performance.

Test Selling New Products

Marketing may decide that a new product will sell, but they will be the first to admit that they don't know for sure. That is why test selling new products is an important concept I'll cover in this chapter. You need to know how to use your sales force to test.

The only way to truly know the success of your new products is to test several variations of price points, benefit statements or markets to see what works. Here's the secret that most companies miss: *always* test with your best people. This way you will be sure that the test is accurate. If your best people can't sell it, it probably is a dud. If it sells like crazy, then everyone else on the team will want to sell it, too. You will want to do all your testing with the same team. Make it clear to the company and The Inner Circle members involved that they are on a special assignment—and pay them well for their efforts. By presenting product or price testing as an exclusive privilege, it will be perceived as a sign of success.

In summary, you can easily beat brick-and-mortar-based call centers. Your staff works hard, spends no time commuting or socializing, and they love to work from home.

One quick story to illustrate this point: I was scaling our radio budget, and I realized that lead flow would increase more quickly than I could hire new staff. So I brought in a call center to take overload calls. It was an excellent call center with a great reputation. Their people were smart and did well overall, but even after weeks of training and drilling, they never performed at the level of my Sales Superstars.

You can build a killer sales force virtually that beats physical call centers any day of the week as long as you are hiring the best Sales Superstars in the country, provide them with the right systems, and train them well. You'll have that competitive advantage if you follow the hiring, training and systems guidelines in this book.

Would you like to learn the entire Superstar hiring process from me? Go to <u>www.InvisibleOrganization.com/Resources</u> and start with an assessment.

The Secret to Reach 95% of the Population

Marketing is *the art of building a relationship with your customers* (as discussed in chapter eight). So what better way to build a relationship than to "talk" to your target prospect five times a day? Did you know that 95% of the population listens to the radio every week? But you may say, "Radio is for big companies who have money to burn on building their brand. It's not for my company."

Spending money on radio for the sole purpose of building your brand is certainly not what I recommend. It is much more effective and profitable to use radio advertising to reach the targeted market you seek while at the same time building your brand.

Radio advertising is not as expensive as most people think. Here is how you can get national airplay: you can buy a single one-minute spot on several different SiriusXM stations for $60 or less each. You may think, "In that case, we can do radio ads and have money pouring into our company." Well, it's not that simple, because without the infrastructure, systems and strategies explained in this book, you're probably just throwing your money away. It won't work.

How Radio Can Bring You Buyers Faster Than Any Other Source

When used carefully, radio can be the secret weapon to make a company's sales explode through the roof in thirty days. It can be a hugely profitable way to increase your revenue—but only if you know how to monetize this tricky medium like an expert.

Most small companies have practically abandoned radio, turning radio into the domain of the large advertiser. The opportunity radio presents is similar to the opportunity direct mail presents—it's an over-used relic of the last decade that has sprung back to life as broadcasters break through the stodgy, jingle-driven business they maintained for decades.

With a tiny budget, just a few hundred dollars a week, you can use radio locally to bring in more patients, more store visits, and even more web traffic. You don't have to be a huge enterprise to take advantage of this strategic marketing tool.

How do I know all this? It's because I ran millions of dollars of nationwide radio ads for Tony Robbins and Chet Holmes over five years as the CEO of Business Breakthroughs. I learned many of the dirty tricks that both stations and agencies can play on you when you are not paying attention. I want to peel back the invisibility cloak and show you how it's done from a client's perspective, so you can skip the learning curve and be successful quickly.

If you currently aren't advertising on the radio or if your campaigns aren't making you money, this chapter can help you "up" your game and get better results. You'll learn how to develop a solid and effective marketing campaign and how to optimize your radio advertising. You'll be excited to discover how to get the most out of your budget, your sales team, and the technology you use.

Don't delegate radio advertising to one of your Vice Presidents unless they already have experience buying and deploying radio budgets. Do it yourself and learn how it works first before you delegate. Stay in control because, as you will soon see, if not done properly, it can cost you a small fortune. From my perspective, if the CEO's job is to grow the company, then focusing on your radio campaign is an excellent use of your time.

Radio is more versatile than most people think. There are different forms of radio: traditional broadcast networks, satellite radio, Internet radio, cell phone broadcasts, podcasts, and non-traditional media.

It's not easy to decide where to focus your advertising dollars. That is where a radio agency comes into play. An agency is like a broker who works for you by finding opportunities, negotiating the best prices and coming up with new ideas to make you successful. Placing ads and facilitating marketing campaigns is an agency's specialty. They know how to maximize your marketing budget, because this is what they do every day.

The right agencies provide valuable services like crafting a radio or TV marketing plan for you and finding the best service providers. Some agencies have more options available than you may realize. Unless you are Tony Robbins and have massive credibility, it's best to use celebrity voice talent to connect with your prospects.

The Voice of Your Company

It's likely that you are not well-known to the general public, but television characters like Captain James T. Kirk of the starship *Enterprise* are. My good friend Fred Catona, who is the CEO of Bulldozer Digital, a direct-marketing agency that specializes in radio advertising, was hired by Jay Walker, the founder of Priceline.com, to promote his crazy idea to build a company around complex behind-the-scenes bidding to get lower prices on travel and hotels.

Fred decided to take the same path many TV advertisers had in the past: hire a celebrity spokesman to represent the brand. He found William Shatner living in his pool house while renting out his main residence, which he could no longer afford. Fred hired Shatner to be the voice of Priceline. com.

While I can't disclose the exact amount Fred paid Shatner to be the voice of Priceline.com, I will say it was initially under $10,000. Later, as the brand started to take off, Priceline. com awarded Shatner a lot of common stock, enough, had he held it long enough, that it would have been worth half a billion dollars at its peak. Priceline.com started on the radio, as did FreeCreditReports.com. Fred launched both and is still involved in cutting-edge projects of similar magnitude.

A celebrity voice, the *right* celebrity voice, took this little Internet startup to places "where no man had gone before" and stands as one of the most celebrated startup stories to this day.

Known celebrities can be paid less than you might think. When starting a new campaign, you are in a good nego-tiating position to secure professional talent to read two sixty-second spots, which you can test for a few thousand dollars. If your spots prove to be successful after the testing phase, you won't mind paying more. Just make sure that you negotiate the contract in advance if the initial spots are successful. You don't want to be charged ridiculous fees if your spots become big and then have to switch to another celebrity.

Most agencies have a long-term relationship with their net-work partners, and you'll be able to take advantage of their buying power. In return they collect 15% commission on your ad dollars. (The commission can vary.) They want your ads to be successful so that you will increase your ad budget. Negotiate with them and challenge them to come up with new ideas. Make them work for you. Get them to record several trials allowing you to hear what your ad will sound like. Be vocal about what you know will work for you.

Don't think: "They know better." They don't, and the best agencies will tell you that honestly. They can never know your business as well as you do. You are paying the bill—make sure you are getting what you want. Don't let anyone sell you on "brand building." Some agencies may try and dissuade you from measuring results. Resist the "fancy talk" and force them to focus on your main objective...to generate revenue—actual sales! Results are always the bottom line. A great agency will support and aid you in measuring results to achieve this.

Agencies have access to detailed reporting from their networks. They typically employ an analyst on staff who can provide reports for you in any format you request. Your own virtual call center will give you a lot of data about your callers as well: the phone number dialed, the caller's phone number and call time, how much time each call took, etc. Always measure the effectiveness of your advertising.

Encourage your agency to present new ideas every few weeks. When you are willing to experiment with about 20% of your budget and carefully consider and evaluate each new idea, you may be surprised what can happen. One time my agency suggested testing Classic Rock stations. I thought that it was a bit odd. Our spots started with the words "Attention CEOs!" because our "avatar" was the CEO of small-to-medium-sized companies. After listening to their advice, there was some interesting logic behind it, so even though I didn't think it would work, we tried it anyway. It worked quite well, because it turned out that CEOs in their fifties listen to Classic Rock stations. In fact, we reached a whole new untapped radio audience.

Don't be quick to throw out an idea. Sometimes you have to test it to see if it'll work.

Optimizing Spot Density

When selecting the stations, an agency uses CPM (or cost per thousand listeners) as their basis of evaluating the "reach" of each station. Reach means how many people will potentially hear your ad. That may be useful information if you're driving showroom sales. It's not that useful as a measure for anything related to direct sales. Ultimately, the most significant measure of an ad's effectiveness is the revenue each spot drives. Figure out how to measure that and stick with it.

Spot times are very important and obviously more expensive during drive time on weekdays. Check the "run reports" (which are reports that show you when each of your spots actually ran) and hold your agency accountable. Let them know you are only paying for the spots that run at the time you specified.

Spot density is also something you have to closely monitor. This is when your spot is sandwiched in between four, five or six other spots. Tell your agency that you want your spot to run first at commercial break and ask them to negotiate with the network for you to get that placement in the spot block. You'll notice that "first run spots" will get you more calls or visits. Will you get first run spots every time? Probably not, but when you do, it will make a difference in your results. It may be worth paying up to 10% more for first run spots.

You may not have to run your spots every day. You should look at your reports and see if you can find a pattern. Are your spots more productive on certain days of the week?

Evaluate your program's success with the help of your agency on a regular basis.

Hacking the Agency System

For every little mistake the network makes, you should receive a "make good," a term used in the industry to appease a client who didn't receive the value he paid for. Never let them get away with even the slightest mistake without getting something in return.

Sometimes political events or breaking news will screw up your position on the pre-set broadcasting schedule. Don't be forgiving. Raise some hell. It's your money and your company. If your spot ran late, if they failed to announce you, if you were bumped or pre-empted (someone else "more important" than you was inserted into your scheduled time slot), or if your spot was cut short, then your losses are more than just the spots that didn't run. Your sales force is lined up and can't be on the phone with prospects if a spot is about to run. Demand that your agency fights your battle, and let the network know about your losses so that you get more "make goods" to compensate. If you have to, arrange a personal call with the network executives to let them know who you are that you're not happy.

In many cases, good clients get "Run of Network," which are remnant spots that didn't sell, most of which you wouldn't want to buy anyway. They may run at 2:00 a.m. or on the fishing channel at noon. They are often on stations whose audience is not your target market. The network sometimes markets them as a high reach, low cost strategy. In general they are used as free giveaways, but if they are sold, they should be very cheap. Sometimes they're allocated to the network's best customers. Sometimes they're used to boost results when a new client is testing a station or a network. Just be aware that they exist and pressure your agency to get your share.

Sometimes, if you are trying to determine true cost per caller, you will have to tell your stations *not* to award you remnant or Run of Network spots because they will skew your results, making your cost appear lower than it really is. This only helps the network prove to you how many leads (calls) you are getting, but it says nothing about the quality of those calls, which will obviously be lower if they are from untargeted sources.

Finally, there's one type of inventory that most networks don't want you to focus on. It's called "Remnant Radio." Remnant radio spots are bulk spots sold to resellers when they weren't successfully sold by the sales force. These brokers or resellers fill an important role in the radio food chain. They are the bottom feeders. Without them, like any ecosystem, we would be in trouble. They take the unsold inventory and find buyers who can make good use of it.

The agency you work with should have a strong network in the world of remnant radio and other "exotic" options. You could end up on big-city stations for 90% less than their "rack-rate." When you get them, you might notice a delightful spike in your call volume and wonder where that came from. Take a look at your reports. When you see a large inflow of calls at an unexpected time, they may have been from your remnant radio campaign placing you on a big city station. It's a gift! Enjoy it.

The argument against using remnant radio spots is that they are unscheduled. Your best, most productive reps use the time between spot times to call prospects. They want to be free when the phone rings and the next wave of incoming calls hits. They organize their workday carefully and don't like unscheduled spots interrupting their workflow. Remnant radio works against those careful planners and can randomly bombard your call center with traffic they didn't expect. It's not a bad thing. It's just something you have to be prepared to manage. Remnant campaigns can be highly productive.

Using TV Inexpensively and Effectively

As you can imagine, the cost of producing a full sixty-second TV spot can run into the millions. But if you are getting good results with your radio campaigns, there is a way to easily leverage that success on TV. Take your best performing radio spot and create a PowerPoint slide show around your product or services. Then overlay it with text and your 800-number to create a TV spot. It's inexpensive, and if done professionally, can pull quite nicely. We used it for remnant cable TV, and it worked great to drive down our cost per lead. Sometimes you may hear prospects or clients say that they saw your commercial on one of the more popular TV shows. That's the beauty of remnant TV. You never know when or where it's going to run. Don't be afraid to test, test, test! The results may surprise you.

Maximize Your Marketing Dollars

I learned how to squeeze every dollar from each spot by relentlessly following up on every lead we received. In most cases, failure to maximize marketing dollars is the result of poor follow-up.

From my experience, it's mostly due to the inefficiency of a company's internal lead-tracking systems. Salespeople don't always want to work on what they consider "old" leads. While the "true gold" lies in new, incoming leads, veteran salespeople know that existing leads are still viable and just need to be cultivated. When properly cultivated, this can make the difference between profit and loss for a company.

Use your CRM system to send creative and informal emails to prospects allowing them to learn about you, your product and services. This builds respect over time as long as you send them quality information. Then when that same prospect hears from your sales staff, they may be ready to become a client.

It's important to understand that leads have a shelf life, sometimes just ten minutes or less. The sales staff knows that there is no 100% connect rate on outbound call-backs to people who have responded to an ad. That is why every business must treat each single lead as the golden opportunity it really is: each lead has the potential to become a lifetime client.

Most business owners calculate the cost of obtaining a lead, yet few think about the value of a lead that has been lost, which could be *much* higher. Even though lost leads can be recovered with some diligence, it's better to manage them properly from the onset, because it's less expensive and more efficient.

IMMEDIATE ATTENTION REQUIRED for This Type of Lead Flow

Most marketing executives and business owners know about marketing and lead flow in general, and they assume that radio leads are just like other leads. This is a huge mistake that can be very costly. Let's review how "live media" lead flow works. It may spark an idea to improve your own lead flow system.

Leads come from various sources: AM/FM stations, satellite radio, Internet radio, and podcasts. It's critically important to understand that radio leads are not like other leads because of the fast response that's required. The best way to convert those leads to sales is by having them talk live to your sales rep.

Have you ever heard a great radio ad that directed you to a website? Did you stop to write it down? Or did you risk your life by going online while driving? Probably you didn't do either one. And if you did pull over to write down the website, did you actually remember to look it up or did you forget all about it by the time you made it to the office? *It is important to keep in mind that people primarily listen to the radio in the car!*

It's a big mistake to send listeners to a website or to give them a phone number that directs them to a recorded message with a website. Most people don't make it to the website, even though they might have been very interested. By the time they get home or at the office, they have already forgotten about you. Likely they didn't even take the time to jot down the webpage, and remembering a radio spot from a few days ago isn't going to happen. Even if somebody does remember, the problem that seemed urgent at the time is likely not at the top of the list anymore.

That is why most companies who advertise an URL stop after a few weeks. The popular brands FreeCreditReport.com and Priceline.com were built entirely on the radio, as I mentioned earlier in this chapter, but it took a massive budget to make their radio campaigns successful. Later they expanded to TV and other mediums of advertising.

The best chance of closing a sale is when two requirements are met:

1. When interest is at a peak

2. When there is a real problem that must be solved.

This is why the *gold standard* for lead conversion with radio spots is to have live operators. A well-trained, skillful sales rep is the best person to convert a listener speeding down the highway at seventy mph from a lead to a client. His job is to find the pain point, which prompted the phone call and then close on the promise of the solution. This is what works. Nothing else even comes close.

Many leads are lost in the first few seconds the phone rings. How can you plug the leaks? Just imagine yourself listening to the radio while driving to your next appointment. You hear something that grabs your attention. You wonder whether you should call or not. "Maybe this can solve my problem," you think and you dial the 800-number-number.

- Scenario a: The phone rings and rings... and rings. You get frustrated and hang up.

- Scenario b: The phone rings, you get connected, and a recorded message tries to sell you something.

- Scenario c: The phone rings, you get connected, and you hear a short message asking you to hold for the next available operator after which they make you listen to scratchy elevator music.

Would you be inclined to wait? You'll likely get the impression that the company is understaffed or just plain disorganized. If any of these three scenarios takes place when somebody calls your 800-number-number, you're wasting money—on the radio commercial, the phone system, and the sales staff. The poor system you have in place is causing you to lose many leads.

Radio leads show up when they do, and they expect *instant* service. The time it takes to connect to your sales rep is critical. There's no excuse for poor execution. Everything I have covered in this book including hiring Sales Superstars, coordinating virtual call centers, and creating seamlessly interconnected networks save you vital seconds.

Your reputation can be made or broken depending on how calls are handled. You can't afford to disappoint callers by letting them go to voicemail and cheating them out of the opportunity to receive the benefits of your products.

When training your sales reps insist on *total* honesty. Teach them that if they don't know the answer to a question to say, "I don't know, but I will get back to you. As a gift for having to wait for an answer, you'll receive a free recorded interview with our founder." This creates an opening for a second conversation with the customer.

If you have a poorly designed system for live lead response, or if you've never done radio advertising because you didn't know where to start, this book should be an excellent overview. If you want to bring in an expert to help you optimize your radio campaigns, send me an email at Mitch@InvisibleOrganization.com.

The Science Behind Fine-Tuning Your Closing Rates

You can't know how well you are doing in any aspect of your marketing without keeping track of your results, obviously. Basic metrics can give you a general idea of how well your spots and sales staff are performing. Using simple tools such as tallying the number of calls from each 800-number-number, the number of calls per spot, the spots themselves, the time slots, and the days that performed the best, you can create a road map that shows you what works and what doesn't.

More sophisticated tracking should be employed to determine the amount of revenue per spot, revenue per 800-number-number, and the revenue generated per day. This break-down can help you see why lost leads are so valuable and why each lead must be protected so carefully. Disciplined collection of metrics helps you gain a very clear picture of lead value and the lifetime value of your customer.

All the systems I recommend have basic metrics built in. All you have to do is customize how you want to see the information reported. Everything becomes much clearer when you can look at all your results in a graphic format. Just as important as measuring is the ability to fine-tune calling queues, voicemail messages, and your script.

There are a number of specific tools to ensure your calls are executed properly:

1. Your call cue and how your reps receive calls should be set up in your virtual call center software. Remember, calls should first be directed to your best reps! Never let more than 20% of your inbound calls go to voice-mail. If they do, make sure they receive a callback as quickly as possible. If you hire staff for an 80% answer rate, you'll feed everyone. A happy, productive sales staff has great morale and makes a good living. Any more than 20% of your call volume going to voice-mail means a lot of leads will be wasted. Any less than 20% of your call volume going to voicemail and your sales staff probably won't make enough money because there are not enough calls to keep them busy and productive.

2. Reduce the number of options callers have to as few as possible. The more options you have, the more

callers you will lose. Never never never let a call go unanswered. Make your voicemail message as clear and concise as possible. Clear means that you can understand what is being said. Concise means that it's short and to the point.

3. Phone menus can have dead ends, meaning the caller is either disconnected or on endless hold when they select an option. These "dead ends" are called "stubs." You must search your system to find them, because your prospects will if you don't.

4. Don't play music for callers on hold. They hate it. There are several options to ease the pain of being on hold:

a. Silence

Believe it or not, callers appreciate silence. They can engage in some other activity while they're on hold. Set up a short reminder every twenty seconds to let them know they are still connected.

b. A recorded message

The message can inform them about a product or service, or it can share a case study with a customer testimonial. Callers will find it worth listening to if they have similar problems they are trying to solve. Provide value, and let them know what their place is in the cue while explaining some of the benefits of waiting.

c. A callback option

Offer to call your waiting prospects back while holding their place in the cue. It works best when the callback is quick. We did this for one of my clients and the results were fantastic. Apple is the master of this. They even let you set your own callback time.

Now let's paint a picture of a great phone answering system. If you took the time to call the 800-number, which of these would you love the most?

• The phone rings three times at most, then a clear-speaking person who is interested in talking to you answers with a warm, enthusiastic, inviting voice, "Thank you for calling. How may I help you?"

• The phone rings once and an interactive voice response system asks you a qualifying question. You comply and are quickly routed to a live person.

• The phone rings once and you hear a recording of how others just like you have solved their problems using this company's products. Then after a short wait you are directed to voicemail with a promise of a quick return call.

This list is in descending order according to what is most effective. However, any of these options are far better than having callers wait forever. Each option preserves tepid callers who are not really sure they want to bother, keeping them involved enough so that they don't hang up before reaching a live person. The goal is to speak to as many incoming callers as possible and call back the overflow calls as quickly as possible. It's critical to call back in two hours or less or the percentage of a successful callback will drop substantially. Balancing staff with peak calling times is often a big challenge. I've developed formulas for high volume call centers and can calculate the optimal number of staff needed for you and your business. Email me at Mitch@InvisibleOrganization.com.

The Foundation of Your Program – Your Sales Script

Obviously the goal is to close as many callers as possible. That is why your sales script must be crafted by someone who understands the psychology of closing your type of clients and knows exactly what your sales funnel looks like. Once your sales script is written, it must be tested. After a day or two of testing, refinements are made and then it's time to deploy it through your interactive automated learning environment to make sure your sales reps know it cold.

It's best to sell a low-cost product, something your reps can close quickly and easily. This becomes your "lead magnet," delivering a powerful benefit to your prospect quickly and generating desire for more.

Using a short sales script can weed out tire-kickers and get seriously interested prospects started quickly. Simply asking one qualifying question up front such as, "Are you the owner of the company?" instantly qualifies your caller. There's your tire-kicker collecting free reports vs. a CEO who has a problem to solve. I wish I had a lobster for every time a rep wasted ten minutes talking to a tire-kicker!

If you have your ideal buyer on the phone, your next job is to collect their contact info so you can start a relationship. After you've accomplished that, go ahead and try to sell something. Why not? You already have them on the phone, and they responded to a radio ad. Find out why they called and answer their questions.

The best script is designed to branch in different directions depending on what the client says and wants. In many cases, when the client describes the reason why he's interested in your product, your sales staff should type in that information to be used later to help close the sale. Or the sales rep can down-sell the caller to a less expensive program or product if they object to your main product offering. Script branches are designed to flow smoothly and naturally, making your sales rep have a meaningful conversation while controlling the conversation very carefully. Your job is to make sure the right product is sold, thus solving the right problem for your prospect. That's how you create a lifetime relationship with clients.

A script must be the right length to be effective. If it's too short, your sales rep won't have time to build a little rapport and find the caller's greatest challenge or burning problem. (The exception would be those companies who use radio simply to get contact information and set up an appointment for a salesperson to call later.) Your sales script doesn't have to work too hard; it just has to close the client on the low-cost "intro" product. The low-cost product should lead your new client to a larger sale. For example, you can offer a webinar for $197 that delivers incredible value to start with, which then leads to a $5,000 sale with a more comprehensive experience.

If you don't have a sales force, now is the time to start hiring. You have your marketing plan, your funnel and your training in place, and you have a great product at a great price and are ready to promote. Plus you have a sales script that will drive callers to buy when your radio ad airs.

We work exclusively with a particular agency that specializes in creating killer scripts for sales teams. Go to www.InvisibleOrganization.com/Resources to find out more.

Seamless, End-to-End Data Capture, Lead Tracking and Conversion

All data from every marketing program must be captured, tracked and closely monitored for effectiveness. This includes the statistics related to all incoming call activity. Good Customer Relationship Management software (CRM) that is cloud-based (like Kazeli, InfusionSoft or Salesforce) can track your sales activity, automate your marketing funnel, and generate the management reports you need to best allocate resources.

Whether you're using an in-house call center where your reps show up for work every day or you have remote staff answering calls from their homes, you need virtual call center software as explained in chapter 5 to handle the traffic.

The Sales Director or Vice President will have to optimize the configuration of the virtual call center. This person plays a key role, because virtual call centers have hundreds of programming options that allow for flexibility of setup.

Your Sales Director will work with the virtual call center support staff to customize the system for your company. The system allows you to prioritize which reps will get the calls first. It may seem unfair to the rest of the team that the first calls are directed to the best closers, but it may motivate them to work harder to get into that elite group. As a business owner, you know that leads are expensive, and you don't want to waste any. Your goal is to maximize your sales.

In Closing

One of the key challenges of creating and running successful radio advertising campaigns is the number of moving elements. Every single aspect is critical and needs to flow to the next step. You must pay attention to every detail. One small misstep could destroy all your hard work and the positive results you previously gained. Simultaneously, one minor adjustment could double your profits. The concepts I've shared with you come from years of experience maximizing radio ad campaigns at every level, from small to large organizations. Using the information I've shared in this chapter, you should be able to minimize losing leads while simultaneously capturing and fast-tracking the most qualified leads.

Turning somebody from a first-time caller to a repeat buyer requires careful planning. When you develop a fine-tuned script, your staff stays on target and can maximize conversion. As part of this process, you may also want to price-test each of the steps to maximize results. The design of each step must be carefully done to move your buyer deeper into your sales funnel.

Overall, to have an effective radio ad campaign, you need a combination of a great script, a top sales team to close and handle objections fluidly, and the seamless technology as described in this book for maximum results.

When done well, live lead flow can provide an immediate, low-cost way of bringing highly qualified prospects directly to your door and ready to buy.

RESOURCES:

Radio Selling Secrets on CD

In this chapter I've shared with you the inner working of great agencies and what they do for their clients every day. Of course, you want to get what you pay for—and a little bit more. Trust your agency but always verify the results. It will make you a better client and make your agency more attentive. This chapter just scratches the surface of how to use radio, which is covered more extensively in my Radio Selling Secrets course.

Take a closer look at the course at www.InvisibleOrganization.com/Resources.

12

Build an Army of Specialists Who Pay You

Timeslips Corporations, the time tracking and billing software company that my partner and I founded, in 1985, became the largest time tracking software company in the industry. Business was booming! Sales kept increasing exponentially. But our success was about to strangle us. We had so many customers that our tech support center received over 3,000 calls every week.

Adding more tech support staff would require more sales to cover the cost, but that would also put more strain on the already overworked support center, and we had already maxed out our sales channels. On top of that, our big customers were demanding live assistance. They wanted on-site help to have our software installed and their staff trained. We couldn't afford to add more tech support staff, and we certainly didn't have the resources to send our staff into the field. It was a catch-22!

For weeks I was tossing and turning, constantly wondering how I could increase revenue and solve the support issue. No solutions came to mind. I continued to be stumped. Then one day I woke up inspired. The answer hit me, and it was so simple! I had found a way to increase tech support, and it wouldn't cost us a dime. What's more, the answer I woke up with that Saturday morning could literally add 6- or 7-figures to *your* bottom line with hardly any investment, as it did for us.

The idea itself was simple—very simple. Like most business owners, I initially thought I had to do it all by myself. It wasn't until I realized the secret of using *leverage* that my business exploded.

The way to achieve unlimited success was to create an opportunity for other people in which there would be a win/win/win situation! It took a year to execute and successfully implement the idea. There were a lot of problems and bugs that had to be solved. And now, instead of stumbling your own way through the same process, you can take the fast track to greater success by benefitting from my experience.

The Idea: An Expert Network!

The idea was simple yet brilliant! Over the years, we had built a database of many happy clients. We leveraged their skills and expertise and launched an Expert Network—*The Certified Consultant Program!* By giving our most experienced users the opportunity to be trained and become certified consultants, we were able to fill the need for more tech support without having to invest a dime. On the contrary, they paid us.

We sent a letter to our entire customer list explaining that we were looking for the top 1% of our most experienced users to become Certified Consultants. Enrollment would cost $995. In order to qualify, they would have to take an exam. If they passed the exam, they would be certified as a Timeslips Consultant. If they flunked, $750 would be refunded.

Hundreds and hundreds of people applied. Wow! What a reaction! We were excited about the huge potential. But like I said before, even though the idea was simple, it took months to implement it successfully.

The first time we sent out the exam, 80% of the candidates failed. So we created a study guide. The second time we sent out the exam, 10% more passed. We were happy with the results from the second exam, feeling that we had selected the best and most qualified people in our network.

The selected consultants received a training binder much like a complete franchise trainee kit with instructions on how to become a professional consultant. It was packed with information about how to run all aspects of their business: how to train office staff, the steps required to install remote systems, and the initial start-up items required before launch.

There were far more details involved in training Certified Consultants than we ever could have imagined. We continued learning and improved our training based on the feedback we received. We discovered that we needed to educate them not only on our software, but also on how to dress, and the importance of brushing their teeth and smelling nice. Looking back I can laugh about it, but at the time it was a very challenging and frustrating process to put all the systems, policies and procedures in place.

Our New Profit Center

The results were amazing! Surprisingly enough, it had not cost us a dime. Within one year:

- We had dramatically reduced the cost of our tech support center since the Certified Consultants were now providing on-site training and support.

- We had effortlessly increased our sales—the Certified Consultants were reselling our products to the clients.

- We had the capacity to expand without adding pressure to the tech support center.

- We had not only solved our problem and increased sales, we had also created a new profit center!

"Show Me The Money!"

This is a breakdown of the revenue we generated with our Consultant Network:

1. The initial fee

The initial fee to join the program was $995. Every year 200 candidates applied, 30% of them passed. Those who didn't pass the qualification exam were refunded $750.

60 candidates who passed x $995	$59,700
140 candidates who didn't pass x $245	$34,300
Revenue from the initial fee to become a Certified Consultant	$94,000

Ongoing training

In the third year we launched the four-day Certified Consultants Symposium to provide the consultants extensive training. Every consultant was required to attend at least once every two years. They asked us if they could bring other people from their companies for an additional fee. Several of them became Certified Consultants themselves. Plus, because the symposium was so invigorating, we saw a huge spike in sales for several weeks after.

Revenue from the symposium (200 x $500) $100,000

2. Recertification

If they didn't attend that year, the Consultants still had to pay the yearly recertification of $500. On average 100 consultants paid for the recertification a year.

Revenue from recertification (100 x $500) $50,000

3. Training materials

When the Certified Consultants provided on-site training at the client's facility, they had to buy the workbooks from us for each person that attended. The workbooks were professionally printed and bound. (The price was low enough that duplicating wasn't worth the effort). We sold over 2,000 workbooks a year and made $35 per book.

Revenue from the workbooks (2,000 workbooks x $35)	$70,000
Yearly revenue from the Certified Consultants Program	$314,000
Estimated additional sales from Certified Consultants	$500,000
Reduced cost tech support center:	$86,000
Total Additional Revenue:	$900,000

The process of setting up the Consultant Network taught me a lot. If I look back on it now, I can spot even more lucrative opportunities for extra streams of income:

• Offer different levels of certification

By creating different levels of certification, we could have charged higher level consultants more to work with larger clients.

• Referral fees

We could have tracked referrals. (It was too complicated for us at the time, but with current tracking tools it's very easy to do.) Another option could have been to charge consultants to subscribe to a referral network. This way, we could have gotten paid for our referrals without having to track their earnings.

• Template websites & email marketing

We could have charged a monthly fee to set up and maintain a template website for the consultants and/or provide email marketing for them.

By the time we sold the company there were over 350 Certified Consultants, and the number was still growing. They accounted for 20% of the sales volume—all because of an idea that didn't cost us a dime.

An Army of Clones

Just imagine the impact that creating a network of consultants can have on your business. You could call it an Advisory Network or a Master Coaching Program. By teaching what you know you "multiply" yourself, enabling your business to experience exponential growth. Think about how much influence you can have by using a network of people to deliver your message.

If you have a business or practice with a product or service and a customer base, you can do this! You don't need hundreds of people to get started. You just need a few good people to build a robust, vibrant network. You could set an initial target as low as twelve people to get started. This will leave you with ample room to grow.

Can you see how lucrative this could be? There are many companies that could build a Certified Consultant or Expert Network program. For example, if your business has developed a unique technique, or if you have a process, method or formula that can be taught and duplicated, you are in the perfect position to build and grow a network.

Your company is a great fit for an Expert Network if:

- *You have a tool (for example, software) that reduces costs, saves time, enhances results, and requires support, customization and training.*

Scott Cook, the CEO of Intuit (Quickbooks and Quicken), implemented the Expert Network by certifying book-keepers as Quickbooks Advisors. They train the client in their office, set up systems, and handle any questions. More importantly, because accountants and bookkeepers are using and recommending Quickbooks to their clients, Quickbooks gains more credibility and has more sales.

- *You've developed a unique process or technique that teaches how to do something.*

- One of my clients taught workshops to help people let go of unwanted emotions. He could only do four workshops a year, because it was a challenge to find clients who could take a week out of their busy lives and travel to Arizona. But once he implemented the Expert Network system by certifying his students as Trainers, he was able to significantly expand his reach—and his income!

- Certified Trainers paid him for the training and cer-tification. They taught the beginners workshops in their home cities. Eventually, hundreds of people took his workshop all over the country, thanks to this core group of trainers. After experiencing the benefits of his method, they were willing to fly to Arizona for the advanced training. Thanks to the Certified Trainers he was able to reach more people with his method, focus only on the advanced classes, and increase his income.

- *You have a medical procedure (dental, chiropractic or surgi-cal) that you've perfected, and you have an invention that goes along with your technique.*

The invention can be anything from a microsurgery tool to a dental procedure. The Invisalign System for braces is a good example of this. Invisalign only works with Certified Dentists who take the prescribed, specific measurements of the clients' mouth, then send those to the factory and make sure the braces fit properly. The dentists have to be trained and pay a yearly fee for their certification.

Other examples are Lasik Surgeries and Fat Removal Clinics. Users must buy the equipment, plus a fee must be paid every time the equipment is used.

When you have a medical device, you can get paid a number of ways:

- Training to use the medical device

- Yearly certification

- Sales of the device

- A fee every time the device is used

It's important to determine beforehand if you have the right type of business and are at the right stage to build an Expert Network.

I have created a simple questionnaire that will help you determine if you have the right type of business to build and run an Expert Network. If you do, there are more resources available that can help. Go to www.InvisibleOrganization.com/Resources.

Hopefully, reading this chapter has sparked creative ideas for your own organization. The above information is just a checklist. There are many more layers and details involved in creating, building, maintaining, promoting and monetizing a network of Experts successfully! You want your network to continue growing for many years and get results for your clients, your Experts, and your own company.

I could only scratch the surface in this chapter. If you're ready to start, allow me to guide you through this exhaustive process. You'll save money, headaches and much frustration by streamlining your learning process and preventing serious errors. Go to www.InvisibleOrganization.com/Resources to enroll in a highly detailed and complete step-by-step course on how to build your own.

On a final note, remember that your skills are unique and people are willing to pay you for your craft. It is a great way to multiply your value. Depending on the type of Network you build, it can allow you to spend your time on more lucrative activities or to select only the most interesting clients to work with personally while delegating others to your Network.

13

Coaches That Double the Lifetime Value of Your Client

Whether you qualify for the Expert Network discussed in the previous chapter or not, there is another incredibly lucrative strategy. It doesn't matter whether you sell a physical product, software, a service or an information product, this strategy can be applied to pretty much any company.

Think about it. As a business owner you are working hard to maximize your sales: you craft your marketing messages to bring out the pain for prospects; you weave compelling stories that educate them and induce them to act by clearly showing how you will alleviate their pain; you write a powerful sales script and fine-tune it with your sales team to increase closing ratios; you do everything you can to hire Sales Superstars and train them professionally. You do all this to make a sale, but what does your company do once the sale is made?

A lot is invested in closing a sale. Wouldn't it make sense to provide products and services that continue to serve your client?

Here's an example: ever since I bought a NuWave oven from an infomercial years ago, I've been using it at least three times a week. It's a fantastic system that allows me to cook frozen salmon and veggies at the same time in just twelve minutes. It blows my mind that the company never thought of offering disposable custom fitted tin foil. All clients would have bought it on a regular basis. It would have been such an easy stream of additional income.

It's pretty unbelievable, considering everything it took that company to get a fantastic product into my kitchen: filling a warehouse with inventory, investing in shooting the commercial, hiring a top-notch pitchman, and spending a lot of money for airtime. Yet after all that, I never heard from them again. It's a big mistake that is costing them a fortune! Imagine the money they are leaving on the table, because they never even tried to sell additional products! (Note: since I wrote this, I now get regular emails from them.) A happy customer is a spending customer, so why don't most companies follow up? Why would someone go through all the hard work of selling a client, a happy client no less, and then ignore him? That's just criminal!

Create a Continuous Stream of Income

The best time to make a sale is *right after* someone bought something. Offering a coaching program allows you to create a continuous stream of income after your initial sale, and it's a great way to improve customer satisfaction. By helping your customers better understand how to use the product they just bought, they will get the most out of their investment. There will be less people who will want to take advantage of "the money-back guarantee," and because coaching is often ongoing, it will become a continuous stream of income—if you build it correctly. A good coaching program is an important piece of a bigger strategy. And because you are offering it right at the time, or shortly after a client purchases your product, your closing rate will be higher!

Let's have look at examples of successful coaching programs:

Real Estate Investment Coaching

You've bought a DVD set that teaches how to buy, fix and sell houses. You have watched them all and now understand the terminology and what you are required to do. But you may have questions and lack the confidence to actually go out and buy a property because you're new and you've never done it before.

When you call the company with your questions, they transfer you to a coach who can help you through the process to get the results you desired when you bought the course. The first two sessions are included with your purchase, but your coach is such a valuable resource that you sign up for the monthly coaching program for $497. You now have a sounding board with experience in real estate investing to bounce your ideas off of, which potentially can save you from making painful mistakes. Even better, it will help make you money!

Photoshop Coaching

You decide to pick up your old hobby after many years: photography. After buying a new camera, you sign up for six weekly classes at a local photography studio to learn how to use Photoshop to enhance your photos.

When the classes are over you have a good basic understanding, but you feel there is more to learn. You are excited to discover that you can purchase a series of webinars you can watch at home. The package includes a coach who will make sure that your software is set up correctly, guide you through the process of setting up your files, and teach you the finer nuances of how to use the editing controls.

Weight Loss Coaching

Your best friend is getting married, and she has asked you to be in the wedding. After looking in the mirror you decide that you need to lose a few extra pounds. Since you don't have time to go to the gym, you go online and buy Beach Body's DVD workout program. When you call to order, they offer a free trial of multivitamins that have fat-burning ingredients for $1 the first month. If you like them, you will automatically be charged $29 to receive a monthly supply.

To help you get in shape, they send you a trial package of protein shakes, and you receive the first month of online coaching for free as well. The coach helps you stay on track with your goals and, of course, will receive a commission if you continue using the multivitamins and protein shakes or if you sign up for coaching.

Business Coaching

Maybe your business has been slow, and you realize that something has to change fast. As you are on your way to a client, you turn on the radio to listen to your favorite music channel. While contemplating how you can increase sales, you hear a commercial offering a free report for business owners, and you dial the number to claim your copy.

The friendly salesperson explains how to get a complete business-building plan if you buy their three-hour webinar for $229. After attending the webinar, you've received so much value that you are excited to buy the $4,000 home study program. As a special bonus they give you four coaching sessions at no extra charge. Thanks to the program and the coaching you have drastically increased your revenue within a short period of time. To continue growing your company, you decide to sign up for the ongoing coaching program.

As you see in the examples above, a coaching program can be offered regardless of the product or service you initially sold. Whether you sell educational programs, exercise equipment, accounting software, or a technical product, you can build a coaching program by structuring a curriculum to better familiarize new clients with your product so they learn more quickly, apply what you teach, and get past the fear of getting started.

Your coaches will work from home, communicating via electronic infrastructure and maximizing their effectiveness, all without a brick-and-mortar investment.

With a good well-written course, the curriculum coupled with four free coaching sessions should guarantee results for new clients. This will motivate them to get ongoing coaching on a monthly basis. Clients will continue the coaching program as long as you provide value.

Don't force clients to buy something they don't need or want by making them sign a long-term contract. When I was running Business Breakthroughs International, many clients remained our clients for years because we provided extreme value and the coaching experience made them more money. We offered an array of the best add-on services as well. Clients were happy to buy from us because we had gained their trust and delivered excellent results.

Coaching can be an important part of your marketing plan to provide an annuity stream by building an ongoing relationship with your clients. It can become a consistent, solid stream of revenue if you follow these steps:

- Master the upsell

- Create a coaching curriculum

- Train your coaches

- Build an elite coaching division

- Track coaching activity

- Set up legal agreements

If you are a coach and want more clients, if you are struggling to get the business part of your coaching practice right, or you want to take your coaching company to the next level, check out my specialized program that teaches you more in-depth how to do this: www.CoachingSystemArchitect.com.

Master the Upsell

A great way to get your new client engaged in coaching is by offering a number of coaching sessions as part of the initial purchase. Don't tell them that the coaching sessions are "free," because this will reduce the value in their minds. Explain instead that the real value of a coach is to get results quickly. Let the client know that you are covering the cost of the first X number of sessions as a "Special Bonus."

Your coaches know these sessions are a chance to prove how good they really are, and if coaches treat these "free" clients like the valuable leads they are, they will lead to more coaching contracts. It is important to understand beforehand that coaches love to coach, not sell. If you want your coaches to close the deal after the free sessions, you will have to make those expectations clear and train them how to sell.

To supplement your coaches' selling efforts, a consultative sales force can continuously check in with clients to make sure they are always happy and satisfied with the products they have purchased.

This is exactly how I helped coaches sell—by building a parallel team of "client service reps" or "business managers" who work alongside them to help build rapport with their clients and assist with closing. We called them our "concierge team."

To the client, their coach becomes their trusted authority and probably will know better than anyone what they really need. The salesperson can upsell clients additional services based on the information given to the coaches. This strategy works particularly well if you have several products that you can upsell. Since all activity is tracked in your CRM software, everyone can see the latest updates real-time.

If you master the upsell, the lifetime value of your client can be substantial. There is no end to the additional revenue you can create. The more your clients trust you and the more positive the experiences they have with your company, the easier it will be to sell them your latest product.

Let's take, for example, the Photoshop coaching mentioned above. The client learns the basic skills in the class he bought and then purchases a three-month coaching program to get personal guidance. When the three months are almost over, the coach offers the next class for advanced Photoshop users, after which the client will need to buy additional coaching so that he can continue progressing. By mapping out a path for your client and providing ongoing value, your income will continue to grow.

Obviously not everyone will buy. Suppose 25% of the existing clients buy the advanced class, which is pretty good. It also means that 75% of your clients didn't buy again. This is where your "client concierge team" comes in and closes more of those existing clients into the next level of service.

But before you can start reaping the fruits of your coaching program, you will have to lay the foundation first. Creating a coaching program will require a lot of effort, time, heart, and soul. Your coaches will be the embodiment of your life's work. They will be the team of experts who will lead clients through the materials you have created and sell them as services, training courses, books, and seminars or webinars.

The Coaching Curriculum

If you have a coaching session with the Genius in an Apple store and you tell him you have trouble using iPhoto, he doesn't just answer your one question. He uses a curriculum to show you step-by-step how to use iPhoto. He has been trained to follow the curriculum, because Apple knows clients will be able to learn the desired skills more efficiently that way.

For your coaches to be successful you need to create a coaching curriculum, a training program, and a tracking system to monitor their learning results. Before you let anyone start coaching, no matter how well they've been trained or how many clients they have coached in the past, you need to ensure every single coach has the processes, techniques and knowledge you want them to teach. In chapter six I go into the details of how to use an interactive, automated training system and show you how easy this can be.

The coaching agreement your lawyer crafts for you should include important key elements to protect you. Please remember that the terms of the agreement will be different depending on whether your coaches are independent contractors or employees.

Before you even start to hire coaches and organize your coaching division, become acquainted with my program at www.CoachingSystemArchitect.com, which is designed to create a large thriving coaching business. Everything in the course is designed based on the concepts of the Invisible Organization.

The Protégé, Mentor and Master Coach

My favorite paradigm is the classic apprentice system in which a mentor teaches his protégé the nuances of dealing with clients, presenting the material, and ensuring success for both coaches and clients. Over the years, I have never found a better way to help new coaches transition from protégé to mentor and eventually to Master Coach or Elite Coach.

The process is simple. As a coaching relationship starts, the protégé is assigned a mentor. A new coach should never contact a new client without the help of his mentor. His mentor is *always* responsible for the outcome of every client engagement. He can assign work to his protégé so that he can manage more clients.

The mentor needs to have the experience of many successful client engagements and even a few minor failures from which he recovered. Since mentors are the equivalent of "Account Managers" in larger organizations, they are responsible for the overall direction of the client assignment, the progress of the client, and their satisfaction.

A suggestion for compensating the mentor for taking on a protégé would be to have the protégé surrender a small percentage of their pay to the mentor for the service of guiding and mentoring. A suggested starting point would be to pay the mentor 25% of the protégé's pay. That 75%/25% split is one of the incentives that make experienced coaches take on protégés.

This payment structure should be set up in the CRM and commission systems in advance so that very little manual work needs be done to pay commissions and shares.

Where Do Mentors Come From?

Mentors are developed from the ranks of protégés who progress as they are actively trained by their own mentors. They do so by working side-by-side with their mentors on client accounts.

Once they become mentor themselves, they'll have the opportunity to make more money as they can now assign work to their own protégés. Using this system, mentors have the tools to build their own company inside your organization.

14

Visualize the Future, You Did It!

"What's the whole point of all this anyway?"

Most CEOs and business owners are very ambitious, passionate, and driven, working eighty hours a week. There is always so much that has to get done. You may dream of success, of making the big money, of the status and rewards of having "made it," and you may be willing to work extremely hard for decades to achieve it, but if you give up everything to get there, is it worth it?

You are alive today! You're in a privileged position. You're smart, innovative, and you're *in* the game. How do I know? Because you wouldn't be interested in reading this book, let alone making it to the end. Postponing life until you've achieved your goals may cause you to miss out on the greatest time of your life—the present moment, today. The time of life is *now*. You are here *now*. You have a family *now*. Your children are only young once. *You* are only young once. You get one chance to leap through this hoop—make the best of it.

Don't miss out on the opportunity to spend time with your family, to cheer your children on when they have a game and to build a relationship with them. But it doesn't mean you can't work hard, be ambitious and make business your primary drivers.

By applying the principles in this book you can have everything you want: success, money, status, and the satisfaction of having your family be part of that journey. It starts with knowing what is most meaningful to you.

Evaluate what is important to you now and ask yourself these questions:

- Do I feel fulfilled?

- How is my physical health?

- Am I taking care of my body?

- Do my spouse and children complain that I'm never home?

- How are my relationships with my family and friends?

- Do I still have a passion for running and building my business?

Since I've been in your shoes, I know how driven you are, how you may be struggling to make the business succeed or fighting to build it further. I made mistakes which negatively impacted my life, my family, and my health.

Smart executives learn from their mistakes. Smarter executives learn from other people's mistakes. Be a genius by combining your smarts and your know-how with the experience of others who have gone before you and have already achieved what you want. Your job is to stand on their shoulders and go to the next level.

Be a genius and think about finding a way to live more of your life with the people you love. Now. Not later. No one said it would be easy. There is a time to work and a time to play. I am not advocating putting off what has to be done if you are in the building stage of your business. It's ok to go back to work after the kids are in bed. It's certainly ok to get up two hours earlier and work. The idea is to use your youth, brilliance and strength to accomplish goals *and* enjoy your life.

When you're older you can reap the rewards of your success while still maintaining your work life. But for now, kick ass and be with your family. Nobody on his deathbed ever looked back on his life and thought, "Oh, I wish I had spent more time working," or "If only I had worked a little harder to get that big prospect to become our client." In the end what matters most is the time you have spent with the people you love, enjoying life together.

Remember that the one thing you can never get back is time. Making small changes on a daily basis can highly effect how much you enjoy your life. I've come to learn that *stress*, if unchecked over years, can destroy companies, families and people. Make the effort to live a balanced life! It's worth it!

Yes, I realize it's easier said than done, easier still once you've already achieved your first couple of million in the bank. Yet how many more zeros at the end of your net worth will pay for a seizure? What is the value of getting to know your kids or avoiding a divorce? No one knows this better than the guy who was so focused on his business goals that he lost his family.

Do you know what your goals are beyond making payroll next month? For me, it was having more freedom: freedom to travel frequently, to provide for my family, and to grow spiritually and emotionally. The goal of this book is to help you work smarter and not harder by using systems and people in the most optimum ways. By carefully crafting fully-integrated and self-supporting virtual systems, you can generate more revenue with less time and less effort, allowing you to enjoy your success along the way. That is the essence of *The Invisible Organization*.

Capitalize on the Lifestyle of the Invisible CEO!

Reading and implementing the strategies I've shared with you should allow you to enjoy more time away from your office, even if you've only partly implemented the ideas in this book. Of course, you are still working hard, but you won't have to show up at the office.

One time when I worked for Tony and Chet, I was in the Sahara Desert in Morocco. I had no cell phone service, but I was able to check in to the dashboard. The management reports showed that sales were booming and revenue was just over the top as my sales team was working on a new campaign. I sent several emails, clarifying the direction of several campaigns and programs, then I went back to enjoying Morocco. That required about ninety minutes of my time. Was it worth it? Absolutely YES! I was able to do that because I am *The Invisible CEO*!

How can you accomplish this same goal? By putting in place solid procedures and systems, by assembling a great management team that fully utilizes those systems to monitor staff, and by building outstanding automated training systems, you can run your empire from your cell phone and laptop.

You can monitor all your marketing and web activity, log into your virtual call center to see every call live, and watch revenue coming in real-time by checking your sales dashboard. Powerful systems and great people make it possible for you to work on your own schedule and your own terms. Even if you started a conventional company but are making strides to go invisible, you will be able to expand your business with fewer distractions, more control, and a real sense of accomplishment.

This doesn't mean you are done. It's quite the contrary. You've just started. You now know how to scale your business quickly (using automated training systems) while adding resources (using a cloud-based environment) without spending cash on capital equipment.

Congratulate yourself for taking the risk to go forward in a different direction, a proven path that releases your pure passion for your clients. Everyone you hire from this point forward is someone who will grow more loyal to you and your company because *you* did what so few other companies are willing to do: you invested in their futures, too.

As you move more and more of your operations into the cloud, hire professionals who value working from home, and shift your overhead from the expense column to the bottom line, you'll be in control of your life so that you can live the dream of freedom and have more of what you want. You'll have the company you always intended to create, a loving family, and you'll be living a happy, rich and balanced life, all at the same time! Sounds like a fantasy? It's not. It's closer than you think.

Let's Say You're Not There Yet

But maybe you are reading this book and feel that I'm describing a pipe dream. You can't see how you could create an Invisible Organization—and maybe one day even have a company that's worth selling. I get that. I've been there, and it's worth doing whatever it takes to make it happen. Reading about the end goal should motivate you to grab the brass ring. If you sincerely believe in yourself, your company and your team, then you can get there with hard work and with help. Always ask for help. You never get anything unless you ask.

You may have to raise money to reach your goals. Many companies must raise money, and there are many ways to do so. It's certainly not simple, and there are trade-offs you must consider. I built my first company without any investors. That was an advantage since we made a profit the second month we were in business. We were willing to go slow and to spend only a percentage of what we made.

Nowadays, many CEOs have to go fast. Competition is there to "motivate" you to get to market quickly with the best product possible, and that means grabbing the lead position as soon as possible. This requires money.

I've been in the position to invest in several startups, and I've run venture-backed companies. Raising money can be a full-time job!

On www.InvisibleOrganization.com/Resources I have resources that may help you better understand your options when it comes to raising money for your company. I have found that understanding the process and asking the right questions can help you realize your goals and expedite the process.

Selling or Merging Your Company

People sell their companies for various reasons, but in most cases they want to unlock the value they have built over time. For years I was cash poor and equity rich, which was a motivator for me to sell. Had I run my company more virtually, more invisibly, my partner and I likely would have had more profit to share and would not have felt as much pressure to sell. The Invisible Organization that you are building will run so efficiently that you will enjoy the benefits that selling may bring in the long run today.

What could be the motivation to consider selling? That's a very personal decision. My partner's motivation was to have more time and less pressure. We started to look for a buyer three years before we actually sold. While profitable and growing, my partner wanted to move away from the day-to-day activities of the business and also wanted to unlock the value he had in the business. We brought in Venture Capital to buy his half, but since they offered him a very low number, I thought it would be tragic for him to part with his hard-earned equity for so little payout. That's why we moved toward selling.

The best way to prepare your company for rapid growth and a clean, easy transaction is to have as much of your infra-structure invisible as possible. If you follow the roadmap of this book, you can have fewer physical operating assets in areas where they are not needed.

Simplistically, all you would have to do is assign your pass-words to the new owners, sign the contracts and rights to your products over to them, introduce them to your staff, and cash your check. I am over-simplifying this process, but there is a point I want to make. Potential acquirers will do their due diligence when they consider buying a company, and if ownership is not clear, it can kill the deal. If you paid a sub-contractor and didn't ask him to sign a "contractor for hire" agreement, you may experience a delay.

When I sold my company, the buyer requested releases from every person who had ever worked on the development of our software products. We had hired programmers in the Ukraine for a short period of time, and we had to contact them to get signed releases. Luckily there were only a few of these loose ends. The same goes for technical documen-tation, engineering drawings, or any work of art that has a connection to your product. If you prepare in advance for requirements like this while you are still building your company, when the time comes for the dreaded "due diligence" cycle, it can go smooth as silk. When that happens, everyone wins.

For example, let's say two airlines want to merge. Besides the physical assets (planes, hangers, equipment, terminals, and vehicles) they each have people working at their call centers. The new owners will take the best of each company and merge those ideas, technology and procedures to make the operating efficiencies work across both airlines. If both airlines have a physical call center, there will be much reorganizing involved: staff may have to relocate to another city to work in the new facility, yet the lease of the building may still have to be paid for several years.

Isn't this a great example of the tail wagging the dog? Their focus had to be "Which building should we keep?" and "How can we herd our entire staff into one location?" With your virtual infrastructure you instead say "Let's keep the best people and elevate them to their full potential!" Obviously, the acquisition will be much more effortless when the entire work force is virtual.

Another example is from a client who owned a meat packaging business. They had a physical facility with hundreds of employees. They were running out of space and were about to move to a bigger facility.

Sure.

Then they realized how they could make their sales, customer service and accounting staff invisible, and thus stay in their building. This saved the company tens of thousands of dollars every month, as they didn't have to move everything, including the refrigerators, cutting equipment and all the EPA approvals they had obtained over the years.

They were able to keep their lease. If they had moved, not only would their lease payments have been higher for the bigger building, but they would have had to continue paying rent for the old building unless they'd found a sub-lessor to take over the lease, which wasn't likely. In addition, their staff became much more productive. They loved working from home and didn't mind answering emails after their regular work hours.

Making your company more invisible will pay big dividends now and even more later when you consider merging or selling.

Positioning Your Company to be Acquired

As the saying goes, "Beauty lies in the eyes of the beholder." In other words, your company will appeal to different people for different reasons. So put yourself in your potential buyer's shoes. By understanding the thinking process of your potential buyer, you can position your company to get the most money out of the deal. After all, in the end you and the acquirer will together determine the value of your company.

Most likely you'll think it's worth more than your acquirer will be willing to pay. Investopia.com offers a valuation tool that calculates the value of a company's assets, like market leadership, branding, active client base, etc. It basically tells you how much cash you would get if you were to sell everything. These types of valuation tools are negotiating points and are not relevant to the actual value of a company.

What really matters is how much an acquirer is willing to pay. Microsoft was willing to pay $1 billion for a company that was generating just a few million dollars in sales because the technology was pivotal to Microsoft's strategy for the future.

Investors are typically visionaries with an eye on the future. They want aggressive returns quickly and therefore will be more interested if your company is growing rapidly. The "book value" the Chief Financial Officer often uses is not very relevant, even though potential buyers may want to use it to negotiate the price down.

Keep in mind that your competitors can be potential buyers, too. If you have a strong competitor, taking ownership of your company can be an excellent strategy to increase their market share while expanding and strengthening their own company.

Another concept you've probably heard of is *the roll-up*. You can decide that it might be more profitable to "roll-up" all your competitors into one giant organization capable of dominating your niche market. Sometimes buyers become aggregators and buy your company by swapping your assets for shares of a larger group of companies of which yours will be one. This means that you can trade your company for a portion of the combined equity in a larger enterprise.

This may or may not involve any cash for the owners. An example of a holding company is Yum Brands. They are the holding company that owns Kentucky Fried Chicken, known as KFC, and they also own Taco Bell, Pizza Hut and other restaurant businesses. Yum itself is not a "brand' since they don't have a product or a restaurant chain called Yum. Yum believes that the combination of their multiple chains is worth more than if each chain were a stand-alone. By having similar companies with a single owner, services such as H/R, accounting and advertising can be shared, and the combined buying power can reduce costs.

Deciding if your company should be combined into a larger entity depends on the possible synergy that could be created by being part of that larger organization. It could make your company assets many times more valuable. Some potential acquirers are interested in dominating a market. If there are five brands that exist in a market and you aggregate three of those, you could dominate that market and make the other competitors irrelevant. If a larger organization comes along and wants to own your niche, they are going to want to buy the market leader and will be willing to pay more for it. It requires knowing your market, your customers and being able to predict the future to some small extent.

The more educated and knowledgeable you are, the stronger your negotiation position will be regardless of who the potential buyer may be. Thus, there are certain key terms and financial concepts that you definitely need to understand, especially before dealing with banks and investors. If you can't talk the lingo or understand the jargon, you will be at a disadvantage.

Potential acquirers use standard reporting models to evaluate your business. The three primary financial statements they will review are: the Cash Flow Statement, the Balance Sheet, and the Profit & Loss Statement. Having tons of positive cash flow makes your company very attractive to potential acquirers. If you have more liabilities than assets, your company becomes less attractive.

Does your company make a profit every month, quarter and year, or are you losing money? The profitability of your business is a key factor a potential buyer will assess. Company valuations always factor in profits, particularly public companies that are driven to deliver ever increasing profits to propel their stock price. That is why it's important to understand what your acquirer is looking for. Some may be looking for product lines to add to their own lines while others are looking for economies of scale, which means combining parts of your business with theirs in order to save money. Others may want a shortcut to development of a new technology you've already perfected.

The reasons to buy a business vary. If your buyer is looking for profitability, you may have to change how you operate your business or adjust your accounting methods. When running my software company, my focus was growth. I reinvested most of our profit in marketing and sales in order to bring in more revenue the next year or two. So when a potential buyer evaluated our profitability, we couldn't show much because at the end of each year I used it all on marketing, thereby reducing taxes and supporting future growth instead of taking distributions as the owner. By understanding what my potential buyer was looking for, I was able to show him the profit a few quarters later by shifting how I made those marketing investments.

When you are preparing to sell, you want to put your business in the best financial position possible. By doing so, you'll create greater leverage in the negotiation process.

- Keep your debt very low or totally eliminate it.

- Keep your operating costs low to focus on generating a higher profit margin.

- Create long-term stability.

- Build longevity (The number of years in business shows how much your clients love you.)

- Keep focused on what made you successful and add product or service lines carefully and slowly, testing each to insure a successful launch.

Key Negotiation Points

If you know you're ready to sell your company, do your research. Once you've identified potential buyers, study them. Understand what they do, who their clients are, what their motivation is to buy companies like yours, and why they are in business. The more information you have, the better you can position your company to be appealing to them. You can never be too prepared.

The best deal allows you to grow and makes your company more valuable. Unless your business is in trouble or there is an urgent situation that forces you to sell, take your time. Be patient and willing to wait for the right buyer. Know what you want and what your financial goal is before you start negotiating. Be willing to say "no" and walk away from the deal if they don't want to give you what you want. Never rush into a deal.

- These key points are important to know about the deal:

- How profitable is your company?

- How profitable is their company?

- How strong are your financial statements (Cash Flow Statement, Balance Sheet, and Profit & Loss Statement)?

- How much debt does your company have?

- What is your current market share?

- Who are your main competitors?

- How large is the market, and how much potential is there for future growth?

- How much equity are you willing to give up?

- Are you selling 100%, a majority stake or a minority stake?

- What method are you using to determine the valuation of your company?

- What other companies have the potential buyer acquired in the past?

- What method did they use in determining the valuation of the companies they purchased?

- Did they buy the company at, below or above market value?

With a full understanding of the answers to the questions above, you should have a pretty good idea of what your business is worth. If you and your buyer believe together that the sum of the parts is larger than the whole and you each get fair value or better, consider moving forward.

In many cases when a business is sold, there is an earn-out period. During that period you are working closely with the new owners to transition your business into theirs. By definition, this is where you'll earn some or most of the upside of your company when you sell, because in many cases they will offer you an upside potential for helping them make their acquisition successful.

That is why it's important that you sell to the right buyer and build a strong relationship with the new ownership. It's very hard to hand over control to a new owner and make the transition successful if you can't stand him. The same goes for your key management. Help them get to know their counterparts in the acquiring organization. Strong relationships up front make for a more successful and enjoyable transaction.

What I want to convey more then anything else is that your life on this earth is not supposed to be only about work. It's about being a great person. A great human being knows how to balance work, leisure and family. A great human being lives as close to a stress-free life as possible in these times.

The reason you have a business is because you want to create a future for yourself. You may have realized that working for someone else could never make you as wealthy as you wanted in life. So you made the decision to start your own company. Your business is your future, and it is important to care for, preserve and nurture it but.... don't let that future take away your life. Money is what motivates me, too, but not at the cost of my family or my health. There will always be periods of high stress, of risk and of strife, just like everyone else goes through. But my entrepreneurial drive and my desire to enjoy my life help keep me balanced. I want the same for you.

Why the Time Is NOW!

"Nothing is more powerful than an idea whose time has come."

This idea's time has come—and it is spreading rapidly. The trend is accelerating without signs of slowing down. Millions of small and large businesses are enjoying the reduced overhead and safety of keeping their staff working from home, and their staff values the perk. Some companies execute haphazardly when they go invisible, adopting systems that are not specifically for the task or without planning properly. You now know exactly what to do and how to do it.

Use this book as a guideline to prepare your staff for the transition and slowly implement the invisible systems you need to best run your company. The movement has started, but the service providers are still catching on. They need to provide the Internet bandwidth, VOIP and cell phone reception that match our needs. Being able to talk with somebody on the other side of the world for free and see each other is pretty cool, but Skype regularly drops calls or the reception isn't clear. It's still not quite there yet. Sprint had to install a

Microcell in my house because there was no reception. This has to improve or we will always be seeking better solutions.

Make it happen for your company and watch as everything about work changes forever. Enjoy the journey! You are headed to a place where life is richer and more rewarding. Traditional brick-and-mortar companies like Staples are losing sales while more and more offices are vacant. Look around. Change is already happening. Don't ignore it. The world is going invisible. Join the wave, or you will be left behind.

Note: I am continuously updating everything I've written here and consider this book to be the beginning of a dialogue between you and me. All you need to do is go to www.InvisibleOrganization.com and sign up to stay in touch.

You'll also see my product reviews of many of the systems I mentioned in this book along with new systems that have evolved further into the world of *The Invisible Organization*.

Conclusion

Sometimes all it takes to change your perspective is a new point of view. It has been my intention to provide you with that new point of view. If I would have had this book earlier in my own career, I would have been successful much faster, would have enjoyed my life more, and I would have been a better leader, too. My goal for writing this book was to shortcut your learning curve and get you to where you want to be faster while enjoying the journey.

I hope *The Invisible Organization* has inspired you to take action. Even if you are not planning to go invisible right now, there are many strategies you can implement today that will increase your revenue and free up your time. The tools discussed can be deployed internally even before you move people out of the building. In addition, just knowing what's possible in terms of technology and systems will help to expand your thinking and give you a broader perspective whether you decide to expand your company, sell your company, acquire other companies, or just become more profitable.

I want to leave you with a thought that has sustained my professional growth throughout my life:

"No one gets to live your life but you."

The majority of people adapt to their environment: they are called employees. Then you have the rare and special few who mold the world around them to conform to their needs: the entrepreneurs and "intrapreneurs," those who are entrepreneurial change agents inside the corporate environment! They are the leaders.

I believe you were attracted to read this book for a reason. Don't assume this happened by accident. You were destined to find this book, so use it! Mold the world to fit your needs. Do it ethically and with passion, and you will attract others to your cause. The world is hungry for leadership, so do it with purpose and do it quickly. Don't give your competition time to catch up. Move forward now.

Years ago, I was told that salesmen are the most successful people in the world. Even though I've been in sales for decades in one form or another, developing leadership and being a resolute decision-maker created opportunities for me I would have never had as a salesman.

Use this book to create unique new opportunities. You know now what you need to do. Let this education be the beginning of your new path. It will serve you well.

My greatest fulfillment professionally has been helping others achieve their dreams. I love that my work and skills enable others to achieve more in their lives. If you are successful and are well on your way to achieving balance of freedom and time, consider paying it forward. Life is not a zero-sum game; we can share our experiences and learn from each other.

To that end, after attending many mastermind groups myself, I'm now conducting my own mastermind groups with like-minded CEOs who want to create their own Invisible Organizations. I hope someday our paths will cross.

I would like to hear how you've created a more profitable company and how you've enjoyed the years since you've gone invisible. I would love to hear from you if this book has helped you develop your strategy to free your workforce from their stressful commute every day.

Being invisible is being frictionless in a physical world. This simply means minimizing the amount of atoms one has to rub together to get the job done. We prefer electrons to atoms and therefore are more "frictionless" than traditional companies. Being able to operate remotely means more time and money for you, your family and your staff. These are the benefits we all seek.

Some time may have passed since I finished this book in 2015 and the day you are reading it now. The techniques and strategies will be the same, but likely much will have changed in terms of technology and products. That is why I'm providing updated new and exciting information at www.InvisibleOrganization.com. Check the resources tab for my personal recommendations and stay up-to-date.

Consider this book as version 1.0 of a lifelong study. You are entitled to get version 1.1. All you have to do is visit www. InvisibleOrganization.com and sign up for updates.

I also write about the oddities of life, the lessons I've learned, and the paths I've traveled. I would be honored to have you on my list of recipients who receive my occasional missives. Check it out at www.MitchRusso.com.

The other business passion is helping coaches succeed. To that end, I created a program to help coaches grow and be successful. If you are interested in that aspect of my work, visit www.CoachingSystemArchitect.com.

On an artistic level, I am a photographer and traveler. If you are interested in both photographic tutorials, travel photos and stories, check out my personal website: www.LensTraveler18.com.

Finally, if you would like to contact me directly for questions, comments or to share your success story, please write me at mitch@InvisibleOrganization.com.

About the Author

As a child I was a New York City street kid with a flair for adventure. At age twelve my friends and I would cut class on Thursdays to travel by subway to Coney Island, taking advantage of the two-for-one special on all the rides.

In Manhattan I had my first minimum-wage job assembling black lights at a hippie poster store in Greenwich Village at age thirteen. When I was sixteen my rock band played gigs at frat parties and sweet sixteen's along with political conventions. Unfortunately "my flair for adventure" eventually got me in trouble: I dropped out of high school and was addicted to heroin at age sixteen. After eighteen months I completed a resident rehab program and was determined to stay healthy and become successful.

I finished high school and enrolled in the DeVry Technical Institute to learn how to fix color TVs. Thanks to the passionate interest of one professor who saw something special in me, I became enthralled with digital electronics and computers.

After graduation, I was lured into an entry-level position at a Massachusetts computer company by a beauty queen-cum-recruiter that traveled to trade schools looking for recent grads to hire, promising the moon. Shortly after I found myself on the nightshift assembling computer frames at Data General. Fortunately, an influential engineer took a liking to me and realized that I had more potential. He made a phone call and arranged an interview with Digital Equipment Corp (DEC) in the R&D labs.

After four grueling hours of interviews, I got the job. I was very excited. Mr. Bill Angel was the key developer of a new technology—he was using dynamic ram chips to build the memory sub-system for the new VAX 11-780, and I was his junior engineer. The world was hungry for this cutting-edge technology that would allow the increase of the size of the available usable memory without adding pins to each integrated circuit or change the printed circuit board layout. The odds were against us. The chips were new, the technology buggy, and we were novices, but we succeeded! When the VAX was shipped in 1978 it had our memory boards inside.

Years later, the CEO of a major security company offered me an incredible opportunity when he asked me to join him to design the first microprocessor-based, multi-point, networked smoke alarm ever created for ADP. It was an exciting project! I was hand-coding the new Z-80 microprocessor. Meanwhile, I bought my first investment property in Charlestown, MA. Shortly thereafter I bought another property. The real estate market was booming, and I was having a blast.

Later, as the field applications engineer for Mostek, I made sales presentations for the sales force. I loved teaching in front of a crowd and then going back to the lab to solve difficult problems with other engineers. I noticed, though, that salespeople were making a fortune. In a pivotal life moment, I decided to become a salesman, and I approached the owner of the sales representative firm, Bill, for a personal meeting.

We sat down and I told him, "Bill, I have been giving this a lot of thought and I would like to get your opinion. I want to be in sales. I can sell like anyone else on the sales team, and I have the advantage of actually understanding the technology. Do you think you could add me to the sales team?"

I remember the look on Bill's face as he responded, "Mitch, great salespeople are born. They don't come along very often. Stick to being the best applications engineer and leave selling to us." Calmly I stood up and turned to Bill and said, "Thank you for your time." Inside I was boiling.

I was so angry that he'd told me I wouldn't succeed that three words surfaced in my consciousness: *"I'll show you..."*

Later that month I enrolled in the Dale Carnegie Sales training course, which changed my life. I resigned from Mostek and became a semiconductor sales rep for different rep firm while studying at night. I graduated with honors and quickly put my new skills to work.

I accepted this new sales position with a 50% cut in pay and, starting from scratch, I spent fourteen months developing my accounts. Finally, after all those months of hard work, I received my first real commission check for $34,000!! And those checks kept rolling in month after month. Remember, this was in 1982 and I was only twenty-eight years old. I opened bank accounts all over the city to deposit my checks since I knew that my money would be insured only up to $100,000 at each bank. I had a small pile of passbooks in my underwear drawer.

One day I received a report that shipments to my client were refused at the dock. That was the first sign of the downturn in the industry. According to an experienced associate, the slowdown was normal and business would pick up again in about five years. The writing was on the wall for me, in 1984, it was time for a new career.

At that time the IBM PC was starting to get very popular, and I decided to buy one. I started to develop software to keep track of the sample requests I received from engineers at companies building prototypes. . It was fun, and it made the PC useful.

When I submitted the $5,000 I had invested to buy the PC as an expense, my accountant told me that the IRS would not allow it as a valid business deduction unless I had a record of every minute I used it for business—and an idea was born! I could develop software to track time!

Serendipitously, a young couple moved in next door a few months after I had moved to a new house. I met Neil who liked guitar and rock music as much as I did, and we became good friends. One day we had breakfast together, and I shared my idea with him. He drew out a screen design on a napkin. After all, he was a professional programmer with five titles in the marketplace for the Apple II at the time. We had several more conversations, and six weeks later he invited me to come over. He showed me a working prototype written on an Apple II clone in Pascal. I was elated!

Realizing the potential of our software, we started a company together: Timeslips Corp. After six months of development, I left my job to dedicate all my time to growing our business.

Then disaster struck. The IRS changed its ruling about contemporaneous record-keeping. Now we had a fully-developed product that was of no use anymore. Six months of our lives wasted! We were depressed, angry and dismayed, but not for long. After brainstorming for a couple of hours, we came up with another use for our software. By adding just one field to the screen, a client name, the software would be able to track time that could be billed to clients.

In 1984 I visited Comdex, the Computer Dealer's Exhibition and one of the largest trade shows in the world, I introduced our new software to the industry. Neil and I had each deposited $5,000 in a bank account as our entire investment. Nine years later we were generating 8-figures in revenue and had almost one hundred employees. The financial rewards, the friendships, and the countless lessons I learned made all the hard work worthwhile.

After we sold Timeslips Corp. I started investing in small companies while also providing them with business insight and helping them clarify their selling proposition and internal structures. I became the CEO of a local venture capital firm, ran a furniture-shopping business on the Internet until the market crashed, and eventually returned to my roots of helping companies succeed.

Life once again took an interesting turn of events when my friend Chet Holmes called and asked if I could help him recruit salespeople. Using his method described in his incredible book *The Ultimate Sales Machine* I tripled his sales force in six weeks and hired several strong candidates to run the division. When I told him I had completed the project, he asked me, "What am I supposed to do with this $18,000 check in your name? That is the percentage you've earned based on the sales of each person you've hired." I smiled. I continued to recruit salespeople, and I built a recruiting division. At one point we had five recruiters who worked for twenty different clients. Chet's powerful concept about Sales Superstars was so clever, it allowed me to build an entire system around it.

About 9 months later, I became the president of Chet's company and joined in the negotiations with Tony Robbins to create Business Breakthroughs International, which we launched in 2008. We were growing fast. We had a powerful hiring system and a well-designed and valuable product that people loved.

By 2010 our virtual call center was answering over three thousand phone calls a week. Life was good... until disaster struck. Chet was on vacation with his family in Mexico when he had to be rushed to the hospital and was diagnosed with stage four leukemia. After a fierce, courageous battle with the disease, he passed away sixteen months later in August 2012. I was devastated after losing my dear friend of twenty-plus years, mentor and business partner. Earlier that year I was appointed CEO of the company and, despite my sadness; I was enthusiastic to make Business Breakthroughs Int'l a world-class business "university."

Tony Robbins and I met at a hotel in San Francisco to discuss my plans to move forward past Chet's death to achieve our collective goals. Tony loved it, but unfortunately Chet's family had other plans for the company and I resigned.

Today, as I write these final words in this soon-to-be-published book, I am once again building a cutting-edge enterprise with some incredible business leaders while at the same time living my passion of helping other business owners succeed.

My intention for writing *The Invisible Organization* is to provide you with the same tools and strategies that accelerated my growth and allowed me to create a better life for my family and I.

You see, I didn't come from a normal home. I didn't graduate top in my class or go to Ivy League college. In fact, I should have been dead a long time ago. Yet my passion for life, my curiosity about the world, my appreciation for business strategies and technology, and my desire to rise above the modest means of my peers propelled me to blaze my own path in this world. It gives me joy to share my experiences, helping others to find a better way.

Thank you for reading *The Invisible Organization*. If this book has an impact on your life or business, I would love to hear from you. If you think my experiences can help you accelerate your own company, please feel free to contact me. I would be happy to speak on your stage, at your annual meeting, or to motivate your staff, your youth group, or alumni.

Email me your success story, your feedback or your questions. I would very much appreciate hearing from you. mitch@invisibleorganization.com

To your success,

Mitch Russo